DISCLAIMER

The information provided in this cookbook is for informational purposes only and is not intended as a substitute for advice from your physician or other healthcare professionals. You should not use the information in this book for diagnosing or treating a health problem or disease, or prescribing any medication or other treatment. Always seek the advice of your physician or other qualified healthcare provider with any questions you may have regarding a medical condition or dietary restrictions.

The author and publisher of this book are not responsible for any adverse effects or consequences resulting from the use of any recipes or suggestions herein or procedures undertaken hereafter. The nutritional information provided in each recipe is an estimate and should be used as a guide only. Individual dietary needs may vary, and you should consult a registered dietitian, nutritionist, or healthcare provider for specific guidance tailored to your unique situation.

The author has made every effort to ensure that the information in this book is correct and up to date. However, medical and nutritional information is constantly evolving, and the author does not guarantee the accuracy, completeness, or timeliness of the information provided herein.

TABLE OF CONTENT

INTRODUCTION

If you're reading this book, it means you or someone close to you has recently been diagnosed with prediabetes or type 2 diabetes. This news can feel overwhelming at first. You might need to change your lifestyle, eating habits, and social routines, which can seem daunting.
It might feel like these new rules will make life dull and tasteless.

Yes, this new diagnosis will require changes, but this book is here to help. It will guide you through the specifics of a diabetes-friendly diet and help you develop new eating habits. Instead of seeing your diet as a restriction, think of it as a chance for new opportunities. Your meals can still be varied and enjoyable. Following this diet shouldn't take away your joy of socializing with family and friends, nor should it consume a lot of your time, money, or effort.

This book isn't about fancy eating, nor is it about calorie counting or food shaming. It's about making the right food choices, selecting healthier cooking methods, and creating a daily menu that meets your body's new needs.

In just 30 days, you won't need a new meal plan anymore because you'll know how to craft a balanced diet with foods you love that prevent glucose spikes. These small changes in your everyday routine could potentially improve your medical condition and contribute to a better quality of life.

Remember, the recommendations in this book complement the medical treatment your doctor prescribes; they don't replace it.

CHAPTER 1. EMBRACING CHANGE: YOUR HEALTH JOURNEY AFTER 50

One of the health concerns that often arises as we hit the half-century mark is the risk of developing prediabetes and type 2 diabetes. As we get older, our pancreas, which produces insulin, starts to slow down. Plus, our liver cells, where glucose is stored for later use, become less sensitive to insulin. This means sugar stays in the blood longer and can be toxic to our blood vessels.

A CLOSER LOOK AT THE NUMBERS

Nearly 40% of Americans have pre-diabetes, according to the U.S. Centers for Disease Control and Prevention. When it comes to diabetes itself, slightly more than 11% of the U.S. population has it—either type 2, the most common, or type 1. Approximately half of the U.S. population has diabetes or its precursor, whether diagnosed or not.*

Recent studies suggest that the COVID-19 pandemic inadvertently contributed to an increase in diabetes diagnoses. Researchers believe this occurred due to factors like inflammation, stress, and cell death during cytokine storms, although the exact mechanisms are not fully understood yet. Some estimates indicate that 1% to 4% of individuals who contracted the virus were diagnosed with diabetes in the months following acute infection.

Moreover, there's a concerning trend of type 2 diabetes affecting younger populations. While it was traditionally associated with individuals over 45, it's now being diagnosed in teenagers and children more frequently. This shift is attributed to factors like over-nutrition, obesity, and low levels of physical activity.

HOW TO FIX THE PROBLEM

These statistics provide a clear reminder of the critical importance of proactive health management, lifestyle modifications, and regular screenings to safeguard against the onset and progression of diabetes.

But fear not! Armed with knowledge and proactive measures, we can mitigate these risks and lead fulfilling, healthy lives well into our golden years. Through a combination of mindful eating, regular physical activity, and stress management techniques, we can take control of our health and well-being.

https://www.cdc.gov/diabetes/data/statistics-report/index.html

CHAPTER 2. WHAT CAUSES DIABETES TYPE 2 & PREDIABETES

The main reason people develop prediabetes and type 2 diabetes is because their bodies become resistant to insulin or their pancreas may not make enough insulin. Insulin is a hormone that helps your body use glucose (carbs and sugars) from the food you eat for energy.

In a healthy person, when you eat, your body breaks down carbohydrates into glucose, which enters your blood-stream. In response, your pancreas releases insulin, which moves glucose from your blood into your cells to be used for energy. Imagine glucose as the fuel that powers everything we do: it energizes our daily activities, fuels our brain for thinking and problem-solving, supports cellular functions like heart pumping and immune defense, and gives us the boost needed for exercise and sports.

Carbohydrates (Sugar + Starches) = Glucose = Energy

01 While it might seem logical that eating lots of carbs would keep us full of energy, it's not that simple. An excess of simple carbs and sugars in our diet, combined with a sedentary lifestyle, can overwhelm the system and cause our cells to become insulin-resistant. It's like the lock gets rusty, and the key (insulin) doesn't work as well. So, the glucose stays in the blood instead of being used for energy, leading to higher and higher blood sugar levels, which can eventually cause prediabetes or type 2 diabetes.

Glucose = Blood Sugar

02 Another common reason for the development of prediabetes and type 2 diabetes is frequent food intake, especially meals high in carbohydrates and sugars. This constant bombardment of glucose spikes puts increased demands on the pancreas to produce insulin, which can eventually exhaust the pancreas and disrupt the delicate balance of our metabolic system. This malfunction contributes to elevated blood sugar levels, emphasizing that not only what we eat but also how often we eat can impact our risk of developing these conditions.

For effective management of prediabetes and type 2 diabetes, it's advised to stick to three main meals at the same time each day. Experts recommend no more than 4–5 hours between meals. The need for snacks varies; some people benefit from them for blood sugar maintenance and energy, while others do well with just three meals. While there's no one-size-fits-all approach, experimenting a bit can help you discover the meal schedule that suits your health best. *

03 In addition to meal timing, recent studies have shown that disruption of gut microbiota composition may contribute to the development of type 2 diabetes. Therefore, dietitians recommend maintaining a varied diet, which in turn is more likely to support a healthy balance of bacteria in the intestines.

* Continuous Glucose Monitor (CGM) may offer valuable insights that can assist you in managing post-meal blood sugar levels. Since individual responses to food vary, it allows you to understand your body's unique response. However, it's important to note that CGMs are medical devices, and interpreting their readings accurately should be done by a qualified nutritionist or healthcare professional. They are not intended for self-diagnosis.

CHAPTER 3. WHO'S AT RISK?

SEVERAL FACTORS CAN INCREASE YOUR RISK:

Being overweight: Extra body fat, particularly around midsection (waist circumference over 35 inches for women and over 40 inches for men), can affect how the body responds to insulin. A BMI (body mass index) tool helps measure weight, with a BMI over 25 suggesting excess weight and over 30 indicating obesity.

Lack of exercise: Being inactive can lead to weight gain and insulin resistance. The thing is, when people get moving, their bodies actively breaking down glucose to generate energy. It's not just about what they eat; it's about what their bodies already have in storage: liver, muscles, and fat stores. But if you're not getting off the couch often enough, all that glucose starts to pile up, and cells can become less responsive to insulin's call.

Family history: If your parents or siblings have diabetes, you might be at higher risk.

Age: The risk increases as you get older, especially after 50.

Ethnicity: Some groups, like African Americans, Hispanics, Native Americans, and Asians, have a higher risk.

Other health conditions: High blood pressure and high cholesterol levels are also linked to a higher risk of diabetes.

Gestational diabetes: Women who had diabetes during pregnancy (gestational diabetes) have a higher risk of developing type 2 diabetes later.

Understanding these factors can help you make healthier choices to lower your risk and stay healthy!

To keep in shape, it's recommended to get moderate physical activity for 30 to 60 minutes most days of the week.

Unhealthy eating habits: A diet high in sugary foods and drinks and lacking sufficient amounts of vegetables, proteins, healthy fats, and fiber is a risk factor.

Since the disease can develop over a long period without visible symptoms, it's important to assess your Hemoglobin A1c level if you notice one or more risk factors. This test shows your average blood glucose levels over the past 2-3 months.

Here are the categories based on A1c levels:

A1c Level (%)	Category
Below 5.7%	Normal
5.7% to 6.4%	Prediabetes
6.5% or higher	Diabetes

Taking this test can help you understand your risk and take necessary actions to manage or prevent diabetes.

CHAPTER 4. THE JOURNEY OF CARBS: FROM FOOD TO ENERGY AND BEYOND

When we eat carbohydrates, our bodies break them down into glucose, a type of sugar that enters our bloodstream. This process starts in the mouth with enzymes in our saliva and continues in the stomach and intestines. Once in the bloodstream, glucose is transported to our cells, where it is used for energy. Any glucose that isn't immediately needed for energy is converted into glycogen, a storage form of glucose.

Glycogen is mainly stored in the liver and muscles. The liver can store about 80-100 grams (around 400 calories worth) of glycogen, while the muscles can store approximately 400 grams (about 1600 calories worth). However, any excess glucose that can't be stored as glycogen in the liver or muscles is converted into fat, leading to an increase in body fat stores.

When our bodies need energy, such as during exercise or between meals, glycogen is broken down back into glucose to fuel our cells. Glycogen stored in the liver helps maintain steady blood sugar levels, while glycogen in the muscles primarily fuels muscle activity.

The body can deplete its glycogen stores at varying rates depending on activity levels, typically using up about 10 grams per hour at rest and significantly more during intense exercise. This means that from one meal to the next, a substantial amount of glycogen can be used up, creating space for new glycogen storage.

Now that we understand the mechanism of carbohydrates' transformation in our bodies and the chain of reactions they trigger, the following recommendations from nutritionists and dietitians become clear:

01 To avoid excess glucose being stored as fat, it's essential to manage portion sizes during each meal. Think simple: keep your carb servings about the size of your fist to avoid overwhelming your system. For individuals with prediabetes or type 2 diabetes, it is generally recommended that women consume about 30-45 grams of carbohydrates per meal, while men should aim for 45-60 grams per meal. * This helps in keeping blood sugar levels in check and prevents excessive glycogen storage.

02 Now, onto balanced meals! Mixing up your plate with high-fiber carbs, proteins, and healthy fats isn't just good for your health — it helps slow down energy release so, you won't find yourself feeling hungry too soon after eating, and saying no to overeating becomes a whole lot easier.

03 Additionally, staying physically active between meals is crucial for promoting the release of glycogen stored in muscles. Regular physical activity helps deplete muscle glycogen stores, encouraging the body to use these reserves for energy and preventing excessive glucose buildup.

04 Maintaining a 4–5-hour interval between meals allows the liver to steadily release glycogen to meet the body's energy needs while making room for new glycogen storage after each meal. This approach helps manage energy resources better, preventing excess glucose from being converted into fat.

By understanding how our bodies process and store glucose, we can make informed decisions about our diets to maintain energy levels and overall health. Eating in moderation, staying active, and balancing meals can help prevent the development of prediabetes and type 2 diabetes, ensuring our bodies function efficiently without storing excess fat.

FUN FACT:
The brain uses around 20% of the metabolic energy people consume from food.

---

* The American Diabetes Association recommends that individuals with prediabetes or type 2 diabetes work with their healthcare provider to determine an appropriate amount of carbohydrates per meal based on their specific needs.

CHAPTER 5. ENSURE YOU'RE NOT ON A GLUCOSE ROLLER-COASTER: HOW FOOD IMPACTS OUR BLOOD SUGAR

As you already understand from previous chapters, blood sugar levels rise after eating. Managing this rise is crucial for people with diabetes. Let's dive into how different types of foods affect blood sugar and how you can make better choices.

In general, foods high in carbohydrates cause the most significant spikes in blood sugar. These include cereals, bread, fruits, desserts, and sugary drinks, which are quickly converted into energy. Foods high in protein, such as meats, fish, eggs, and dairy products, cause a more moderate rise, while oily foods have the least immediate impact.

Here's a quick overview:

Nutrient type	Examples
Carbohydrates: sugars, starches, fibers	Bread, cereals, pasta, and other grain-based products
	Starchy vegetables like potatoes and corn
	Dairy products such as milk, yogurt, and cheeses
	Beans, legumes, and peas
	Fruits and fruit juices
	Soft drinks and sports drinks
	Snack items and desserts
Protein	Meats, fish, eggs, soy products, milk, dairy
Fat	Oils and fats

But not all carbs are created equal, especially for those managing diabetes. There are three main types of carbohydrates to keep an eye on:

01 Sugar: Found naturally in foods like fruits, honey, and dairy, but also added by manufacturers to products like ketchup and cereals. These simple carbs release glucose quickly into the bloodstream, causing sharp spikes in blood sugar levels.

02 Starch: Present in starchy vegetables, beans, and both refined and whole grains. Starches can act like sugar, but if they are complex carbs, like those found in sweet potatoes, lentils, and whole-grain bread, they release glucose more gradually, preventing sudden spikes.

03 Fiber: Packed into fruits, vegetables, whole grains, nuts, beans, and legumes. Fiber slows down glucose absorption, helping to keep blood sugar levels steady.

Each type of carbohydrate has a different glycemic index (GI), which indicates how fast glucose enters your bloodstream. The higher the GI, the faster the glucose hits your blood, causing sharp spikes.

FOODS CAN BE GROUPED BASED ON THEIR GI:

LOW GI (LESS THAN 40):
These carbs are digested slowly, providing a gradual rise in blood sugar.

MEDIUM GI (40 TO 70):
These foods cause a moderate increase in blood sugar levels.

HIGH GI (ABOVE 70):
These carbs break down quickly, leading to rapid spikes in blood sugar.

Low GI Foods (<40)	GI
Cherries	22
Kidney beans	24
Raspberry	25
Grapefruit	25
Full-fat milk	27
Chickpeas	28
Lentils	29
Low-fat milk	30
Plain yogurt	30
Pears	33
Quinoa	35
Carrots	35
Apples	36

Medium GI Foods (40-70)	GI
Strawberries	40
Oranges	43
Spaghetti	46
Buckwheat	52
Brown rice	50
Bananas	52
Sweet potatoes	52
Corn	52
Bulgur	54
Oats	55
Pineapple	66
Whole wheat bread	69

High GI Foods (>70)	GI
White rice	70
Watermelon	72
Mashed potatoes	75
Instant oatmeal	79
Cornflakes	81
Grapes	59-72
Honey	58-87
Maple syrup	54-74
Rice crackers	91

Opting for healthier flour alternatives, which are often packed with nutrients and feature lower glycemic indexes, can be a wise decision for regulating blood sugar levels and promoting overall well-being. This is especially true considering that the glycemic index of white wheat flour tends to be quite high. So, why not take a closer look at these options?

Type of flour	GI
Flaxseed flour	15
Almond flour	25
Lentil flour	35-45
Chickpea flour	35-45
Whole grain flour	54
Coconut flour	55
Buckwheat flour	65
Rye flour	70
Wheat flour	75

At first glance, it seems logical to favor foods with low to moderate glycemic indexes (GI) and avoid those with high GI to prevent glucose spikes. However, strict diets that eliminate certain foods in practice prove ineffective in the long run as they often result in setbacks and stress.

Moreover, a food's glycemic index (GI) doesn't always accurately reflect its impact on blood sugar levels. This is where the concept of glycemic load (GL) comes into play – the amount of carbohydrates per 100 grams of food. Consider this: a juicy slice of watermelon may have a high GI, but its glycemic load is relatively low due to its high water content. Conversely, a denser fruit like cantaloupe might have a higher glycemic load for the same serving size. Beyond this, factors like processing and cooking methods, dish composition, whether it contains healthy fats, proteins, and fiber, and meal order play pivotal roles in how our bodies process glucose.

By understanding these nuances, we can develop effective glucose management strategies without feeling the need to constantly monitor GI and GL or give up our favorite foods.

CHAPTER 6. HEAT, TREAT, AND GLUCOSE: EXPLORING THE IMPACT OF FOOD PROCESSING ON BLOOD SUGAR

Have you ever stopped to think about why the way we cook our food matters so much? It's not just about taste – it's about how it affects our health too. From heating things up to cooling them down, even techniques like mashing and juicing can make a big difference in how our bodies handle what we eat.

In this chapter, we're diving deep into the science behind cooking methods and food processing. We'll uncover how these techniques can completely change a product's glycemic index and influence glucose spike management.

FIBERS ARE YOUR HEALTH'S BEST FRIENDS

For those embracing proper nutrition and a healthy lifestyle to prevent type 2 diabetes and prediabetes, it's important to understand this: the more fiber in your food, the better. Fiber slows down the absorption of glucose into the bloodstream, preventing spikes in glucose and insulin.

For years, marketing has touted a glass of freshly squeezed orange juice as the ultimate healthy breakfast. But the reality is different. During juicing, all the fiber from the fruit is lost, leaving you with sugary water (even though some vitamins and nutrients remain). However, this juice leads to a quick glucose spike followed by a rapid drop in blood sugar levels. On the other hand, a whole orange with its fiber intact promotes a slower release of glucose, hence having a lower glycemic index. A similar story applies to mashed potatoes versus whole-baked potatoes.

Product Type	GI
Orange	40-45
Orange juice	50-55*
Whole baked potato	50-60
Mashed potatoes	85-90

Therefore, one common and fundamental recommendation is to avoid juicing, meshing, blending, or crushing foods. The less food processed during preparation, the better; this way, fiber retains its structure and helps stabilize blood glucose levels.

Additionally, adding fiber, such as vegetables, nuts, and legumes, to high-carbohydrate foods like pasta or rice can help reduce the rate of glucose release into the bloodstream. Fiber serves as a protective barrier, slowing down the process of glucose release and promoting a more steady and balanced blood sugar level.

* To make a glass of freshly squeezed orange juice, you typically need about 3-4 oranges, depending on their size and the amount of juice they yield. Hence, the amount of sugar intake per serving can easily be multiplied by 3 or 4 compared to consuming a whole orange.

THE HEAT EFFECT: HOW COOKING TRANSFORMS YOUR MEALS

While the number of carbs in your food stays the same, the glycemic index (GI) can change depending on how you cook it. Take carrots, for instance. Raw carrots have a low GI of 35, but once you cook them, their GI shoots up to 75!

When we cook starchy foods like potatoes or pasta, the heat and water cause the starches to swell and soften in a process called gelatinization, this breaks down more complex starch compounds, making them easier to digest and quickly convert into sugar, thereby raising the GI. For example, mashed potatoes have a higher GI because the cooking process makes the starches very digestible.

However, something interesting happens when you let these foods cool down after cooking. The starches begin to re-form in a process called retrogradation, becoming less digestible and thus lowering the GI. As these starches reassemble, a significant portion becomes resistant to digestion and absorption into the bloodstream. These resistant starches are not only beneficial for lowering the GI but also serve as food for the gut microbiome, promoting better digestive health.

Next time you enjoy a potato salad or cold pasta dish, remember that you're not just eating a delicious meal. You're also feeding the friendly bacteria in your gut, supporting a balanced and healthy microbiome!

It's worth noting that when starchy vegetables are reheated, they lose their ability to gelatinize starch. This means that reheating these foods doesn't raise their glycemic index.

COOL DOWN TO SLIM DOWN: HOW STORAGE AND COOLING LOWER THE GLYCEMIC INDEX

Storing starchy foods at low temperatures, such as keeping pre-cooked meals in the fridge, helps the starches become more resistant to digestion. This process is also promoted by drying foods. For instance, as bread goes stale, it loses moisture, causing the starches to become more resistant. The same effect occurs when bread is toasted.

While this change doesn't completely reverse the cooking process, it significantly lowers the glycemic index. This is why spaghetti cooked al dente and then cooled for a salad has a GI of 35. Similarly, bread made from white flour will have a different GI depending on whether it's fresh, stale, or toasted. Even freezing and then thawing fresh bread can lower its glycemic index.

HEALTHIER COOKING METHODS: BRAISING, BAKING, AND STEAMING

When preparing starchy vegetables such as pumpkins, beets, or carrots, the cooking method used can significantly influence their nutritional impact, particularly their glycemic index (GI). Unlike boiling in water, which can cause these vegetables to absorb excessive moisture and lead to a faster breakdown of complex starches into simpler sugars, methods like braising, baking, or steaming help preserve their natural composition.

For instance, roasted carrots retain more of their original starch structure compared to their boiled counterparts, resulting in a slower and more gradual release of sugars into the bloodstream. This makes braising, baking, or steaming ideal methods for those looking to manage blood sugar levels effectively through diet.

CARB MAKEOVER: TRANSFORMING YOUR PLATE WITH SMART ADDITIONS

In our culinary adventures, rarely do we consume foods in their purest form. Cooking often involves blending several ingredients, making it challenging to pinpoint their exact glycemic index and load. For example, add a drizzle of olive oil to rice or mix nuts into oatmeal. These simple additions not only enhance flavor and texture but also significantly slow down the release of sugar into the bloodstream. This practical approach underscores the importance of balanced meal preparation in managing stable blood sugar levels and overall metabolic health.

For instance, can't imagine breakfast without granola? Add it to Greek yogurt and top with berries. Used to having toast with jam for breakfast? Swap the jam for avocado, a slice of salmon, or peanut butter. Love pasta? Mix in some spinach and cherry tomatoes for added nutrients and a slower release of carbs. Enjoy your evening rice bowl? Add some black beans and a handful of vegetables to create a more balanced meal.

These smart additions not only make your meals more nutritious but also help in maintaining better blood sugar levels and promoting overall well-being.

CHAPTER 7. SCIENCE BEHIND TRADITION: UNDERSTANDING THE INFLUENCE OF FOOD ORDER ON BLOOD SUGAR

For generations, our ancestors intuitively started their meals with vegetable salads or appetizers rich in fiber. Now, modern science is unraveling the wisdom behind these age-old practices. Research shows that beginning your meal with vegetables and fiber-rich foods before moving on to carbohydrates like bread or pasta can significantly impact how your body processes sugars.

When you kick off your meal with a colorful salad packed with greens, tomatoes, and perhaps some grilled chicken or steamed veggies drizzled with olive oil, you're setting the stage for better blood sugar control. The fiber and nutrients from these foods slow down the digestion of carbohydrates that follow, preventing rapid spikes in blood glucose levels. This approach not only helps in managing diabetes but also reduces the need for insulin, promoting more stable energy levels throughout the day.

By simply adjusting the order in which we eat, we can instantly reduce glucose spikes by more than 50 percent. This immediate impact highlights the practical advantages of adjusting meal structure according to scientific findings. Understanding this rationale helps us recognize how minor alterations in meal arrangement can lead to significant health benefits. Aligning our eating habits with this knowledge supports better management of blood sugar levels and promotes overall well-being, emphasizing the importance of a balanced diet focused on nutrient-rich foods from the outset of each meal.

CORRECT FOOD ORDER:

1. Fiber (broccoli)

3. Protein (shrimp)

2. Fats (avocado)

4. Carbs (rice)

CHAPTER 8. THE POWER OF SMALL CHANGES

We often fall for the myth that changing habits is a quick fix, achievable in just 21 days. But the truth is that meaningful change takes time and patience. Each of us must find our own rhythm and progress one step at a time.

Healthy behaviors are the daily choices that shape your well-being. This includes monitoring blood sugar levels, eating balanced meals, maintaining a regular eating schedule, staying hydrated, getting enough sleep, staying active, taking medications, and attending medical appointments. These actions form the cornerstone of managing diabetes effectively.

However, making these changes isn't easy. We've all faced the challenge of losing weight, cutting back on sweets, or finding the motivation to exercise. The journey is often filled with obstacles and moments of self-doubt.

The key is to embrace the power of tiny habits. Instead of overwhelming yourself with grand plans, focus on small, manageable changes. Start with a clear goal, break it down into simple actions, and weave them into your daily routine. Celebrate each small victory, and gradually, these habits will become second nature.

Try adopting one new habit each week to make transitioning to a healthier diet easier. This step-by-step approach reduces stress and minimizes setbacks, helping you build sustainable, healthy habits over time.

01 **Start with fiber-rich and protein-packed foods:** begin each meal with vegetables, salads, or protein sources like eggs, fish, or legumes. This not only stabilizes blood sugar levels but also prolongs satiety, reducing the urge for sweet snacks between meals.

02 **Pair carbohydrates with fiber and protein:** when consuming carbohydrates, include fiber-rich foods like vegetables, fruits, and whole grains, as well as protein sources such as lean meats, tofu, or nuts. This combination slows down the release of glucose into the bloodstream and supports prolonged satisfaction until the next main meal.

03 **Stay hydrated:** adequate hydration is vital for various body functions, including regulating blood pressure, body temperature, and blood glucose levels. Insufficient water intake can lead to higher blood glucose concentrations.

04 **Maintain a regular eating schedule:** stick to regular meal times and avoid excessive snacking to prevent frequent spikes in blood glucose levels throughout the day.

05 **Choose whole foods over processed options:** opt for whole fruits and vegetables rather than processed snacks such as chips, cookies, or sugary drinks.

06 **Control portion sizes:** pay attention to portion sizes to avoid overconsumption, which can cause blood sugar spikes. Use smaller plates, bowls, and cups to help control portions naturally.

07 **Incorporate moderate physical activity after meals:** aim for light physical activity after each meal, such as having a walk, doing household chores, or gentle exercises like squats. This helps regulate blood sugar levels and supports digestion.

08 **Prioritize sleep and relaxation:** adequate sleep and relaxation reduce stress hormones that can lead to higher blood glucose levels. Aim for 7-9 hours of quality sleep each night to support overall health. *

By gradually integrating these habits into your routine, you can establish a sustainable approach to eating that supports stable blood sugar levels and overall well-being. As you journey towards better health, age doesn't have to mean decline; it's an opportunity to rewrite the script of aging, unlocking vitality and joy in every chapter of life.

Always consult with a healthcare professional or dietitian for personalized advice based on your specific health needs.

CHAPTER 9. BREAKFASTS TO START YOUR DAY RIGHT

For years, advertising has portrayed an enticing image of the ideal breakfast on TV screens, billboards, magazines, and newspapers: a glass of fresh orange juice, a bowl of cornflakes with chocolate milk, or a cup of coffee with a croissant. However, these options are far from healthy and can even harm your well-being, pushing you toward insulin resistance. After such a breakfast, you might be ravenously hungry two hours later, craving something sweet. This sets the tone for your entire day, leading to constant snacking, fatigue, irritability, and brain fog.

So, what does a healthy breakfast look like? It's all about balancing healthy fats, proteins, and fiber. Think of an omelet with green beans and a small side salad. This kind of breakfast will keep you full and satisfied for 4-5 hours, preventing those pesky blood sugar spikes.

Aim to eat within 1-2 hours of waking up, and avoid coffee on an empty stomach. For those who enjoy coffee with milk and are looking for plant-based alternatives, choose nut-based milk like almond, pistachio, or hazelnut, as oat and rice milk have a high glycemic index.

Remember, breakfast sets the tone for your entire day. Think of it as "dinner for breakfast" by choosing nutrient-dense, satisfying foods that support your energy levels and overall well-being.

Embrace a breakfast that fuels your day right from the start and keeps you feeling great.

SPICY TOMATO EGG SKILLET

NUTRITIVE VALUE PER SERVING:

- **Calories:** 232 kcal
- **Carbs:** 5g / **Sugars:** 2.6g / **Fibers:** 2g
- **Proteins:** 17g
- **Fats:** 15g
- **GI:** Low

HERE IS HOW TO MAKE IT:

01 **Prepare the base:** heat the olive oil in a large skillet over medium heat. Add the chopped onion and diced bell pepper, cooking until softened, about 5 minutes.

02 **Add garlic and spices:** stir in the minced garlic, cumin, paprika, and chili powder. Cook for another 1-2 minutes until fragrant.

03 **Add tomatoes:** pour in the diced tomatoes, including the juice. Season with salt and pepper. Simmer the mixture for about 10 minutes until it thickens slightly.

04 **Add the eggs:** make small wells in the tomato mixture and crack the eggs into each well. Cover the skillet and cook for 5-7 minutes or until the eggs are done to your liking.

05 **Garnish and serve:** garnish with fresh cilantro or parsley. Serve hot.

INGREDIENTS SWAPS AND SUBSTITUTIONS:

- **Bell pepper:** substitute with zucchini (GI: 15), eggplant (GI: 15), or mushrooms (GI: 10) for a different texture.
- **Diced tomatoes:** use fresh tomatoes (GI: 38) if available.
- **Spices:** adjust the spices to your taste or use a premade shakshuka spice blend.

PREP: 10 min   **COOK:** 20 min   **SERVINGS:** 1-2

INGREDIENTS YOU WILL NEED:

- 2-3 large eggs (GI: 0)
- 1 tablespoon olive oil (GI: 0)
- 1/2 onion, finely chopped (GI: 15)
- 1/2 bell pepper, diced (GI: 15)
- 2 cloves garlic, minced (GI: 30)
- 1 can (14 oz) diced tomatoes (GI: 38)
- 1 teaspoon ground cumin (GI: 0)
- 1 teaspoon paprika (GI: 0)
- 1/2 teaspoon chili powder (GI: 0)
- Salt and pepper to taste (GI: 0)
- Fresh cilantro or parsley for garnish (GI: 15)

SERVING SUGGESTIONS:

- Serve with whole grain bread or pita for dipping.
- Pair with a side salad of mixed greens or cucumbers.
- Enjoy with a dollop of Greek yogurt or a sprinkle of feta cheese for added flavor.

PREP: 10 min   **COOK:** 15 min   **SERVINGS:** 1-2

GREEN SHAKSHUKA WITH LEEKS, SPINACH, AND GREEN PEPPERS

Green shakshuka offers a refreshing twist on the traditional North African and Middle Eastern dish. Packed with nutritious fibers and rich in vitamins and minerals, this flavorful meal is a delightful choice for a hearty breakfast or brunch.

NUTRITIVE VALUE PER SERVING:

- **Calories:** 341 kcal
- **Carbs:** 21g / **Sugars:** 7g / **Fibers:** 5g
- **Proteins:** 19g
- **Fats:** 16g
- **GI:** Low

INGREDIENTS YOU WILL NEED:

- 2-3 large eggs (GI: 0)
- 1 tablespoon olive oil (GI: 0)
- 1 leek, thinly sliced (GI: 15)
- 1/2 bell pepper, diced (GI: 15)
- 2 cups fresh spinach (GI: 15)
- 1 green bell pepper, diced (GI: 15)
- 2 cloves garlic, minced (GI: 35)
- 1 teaspoon ground cumin (GI: 0)
- Salt and pepper to taste (GI: 0)
- Fresh parsley or cilantro for garnish (GI: 15)

SERVING SUGGESTIONS:

- Enjoy with crusty whole-grain bread and hummus for dipping.
- Serve alongside a fresh green salad or roasted vegetables for a complete meal.

INGREDIENTS SWAPS AND SUBSTITUTIONS:

- **Leek:** substitute with spring onions (GI: 15) or regular onions (GI: 15) for a similar flavor.
- **Spinach:** use kale (GI: 15) or Swiss chard (GI: 10) instead of spinach for variation.

HERE IS HOW TO MAKE IT:

01 **Cook the leeks and green bell pepper:** heat olive oil in a skillet over medium heat. Add the sliced leeks and diced green bell pepper. Cook until softened, about 5 minutes.

02 **Add Spinach and Garlic:** stir in the fresh spinach and minced garlic. Cook for another 2-3 minutes until the spinach wilts.

03 **Season and Simmer:** stir in ground cumin, salt, and pepper to taste. Cook for 1-2 minutes to blend the flavors.

04 **Add the eggs:** make small wells in the spinach mixture and crack the eggs into each well. Cover the skillet and cook for 5-7 minutes or until the eggs are cooked to your liking.

05 **Garnish and serve:** garnish with fresh parsley or cilantro. Serve hot.

TOMATO AND RICOTTA OMELET BAKE IN A LOW-CARB LENTIL TORTILLA

PREP: 10 min   **COOK:** 15 min   **SERVINGS:** 2

NUTRITIVE VALUE PER SERVING (APPROX. 200 GRAMS):

- **Calories:** 308 kcal
- **Carbs:** 18g / **Sugars:** 3g / **Fibers:** 8g
- **Proteins:** 23g
- **Fats:** 15g
- **GI:** Low

HERE IS HOW TO MAKE IT:

01   Prepare the lentil tortilla:

- In a medium bowl, mix the lentil flour, water, and salt until a smooth batter forms.
- Heat a non-stick skillet over medium heat and lightly grease it with olive oil.
- Pour a thin layer of batter into the skillet, spreading it evenly to form a tortilla.
- Cook for about 2 minutes on each side or until lightly browned and cooked through. Remove from skillet and set aside.

02   Assemble the omelet bake:

- Preheat your oven to 375°F (190°C).
- Grease a baking dish with olive oil and place the cooked lentil tortilla on the bottom, pressing it up the sides to form a crust.
- In a bowl, whisk the eggs with a pinch of salt and pepper.
- Pour the eggs into the tortilla-lined baking dish.
- Evenly distribute the halved cherry tomatoes and dollops of ricotta cheese over the eggs.
- Sprinkle with chopped basil.

03   Bake:

- Place the baking dish in the preheated oven and bake for 15 minutes, or until the eggs are fully set and the tortilla edges are crispy.
- Remove from the oven and let it cool slightly before slicing.

INGREDIENTS YOU WILL NEED:

For the lentil tortilla:
- 1 cup lentil flour (GI: 13-15)
- 1/2 cup water
- A pinch of salt (GI: 0)
- 1 tablespoon olive oil for greasing (GI: 0)

For the omelet bake:
- 4 large eggs (GI: 0)
- 1/2 cup ricotta cheese (GI: 27)
- 1 cup cherry tomatoes, halved (GI: 15)
- 1/4 cup fresh basil leaves, chopped (GI: 0)
- Salt and pepper to taste (GI: 0)

SERVING SUGGESTIONS:

- Serve with a side of mixed greens drizzled with balsamic vinaigrette for a complete meal.
- Pair with a slice of avocado or a dollop of guacamole for added healthy fats.

INGREDIENTS SWAPS AND SUBSTITUTIONS:

- **Lentil tortilla:** you can use a ready-made low-carb tortilla instead of making one from scratch.
- **Ricotta cheese:** substitute with cottage cheese (GI: 27) or feta cheese (GI: 30) for a different flavor profile.

PREP: 10 min   **COOK:** 12 min   **SERVINGS:** 4

MUSHROOM & GOAT CHEESE BREAKFAST BURRITOS

These breakfast burritos are a delicious blend of savory mushrooms, sweet red bell peppers, creamy goat cheese, and fluffy scrambled eggs. They provide a balanced combination of protein, healthy fats, and moderate-GI carbohydrates, making them a satisfying choice for breakfast or a quick snack.

NUTRITIVE VALUE PER 3.5 OZ (100 GRAMS):

- **Calories:** 415 kcal
- **Carbs:** 30g / **Sugars:** 5g / **Fibers:** 4g
- **Proteins:** 21g
- **Fats:** 23g
- **GI:** Medium

INGREDIENTS YOU WILL NEED:

- 2 tablespoons olive oil
- 1/2 white onion, diced (GI: 10)
- 2 garlic cloves, minced (GI: 35)
- 2 cups crimini mushrooms, chopped (GI: 15)
- 1 red bell pepper, diced (GI: 15)
- 8 large eggs (GI: 0)
- 3 tablespoons milk (GI: 30)
- Salt and pepper to taste (GI: 0)
- 4 large whole wheat tortillas (GI: 45)
- 4 tablespoons goat cheese (GI: 20)

SERVING SUGGESTIONS:

- Pair with a dipping sauce or homemade tomato salsa.

INGREDIENTS SWAPS AND SUBSTITUTIONS:

- **Eggs:** Substitute with egg whites or a combination of whole eggs and egg whites for lower cholesterol.

- **Red Bell Pepper:** Swap with tomatoes (GI: 15), spinach (GI: 15), or asparagus (GI: 15) for different flavors and textures.

- **Goat Cheese:** Replace with feta or another cheese of choice, or use a dairy-free alternative if needed.

HERE IS HOW TO MAKE IT:

01 Heat oil in a large skillet over medium-high heat. Add onion and garlic, cook until translucent (2-3 minutes).

02 Add mushrooms and red bell pepper, cook until mushrooms are golden brown and peppers are tender (about 4-5 minutes). Season with salt, stir well, and remove from heat.

03 In a large bowl, whisk eggs and milk. Season with salt and pepper. Cook in another skillet over medium heat, stirring frequently, until eggs are set (4-5 minutes). Remove from heat.

04 Warm tortillas in the microwave for 10 seconds. Lay out tortillas on aluminum foil, spread goat cheese on each. Divide mushroom and pepper mixture and scrambled eggs among tortillas. Roll each burrito and wrap in foil.

05 Freeze burritos in a labeled freezer bag. To reheat, unwrap from foil, microwave on high for 1-2 minutes until heated through.

a great option for meal prep

ZUCCHINI WAFFLES WITH CRISPY BACON AND EGG

These savory zucchini waffles are topped with crispy bacon and a perfectly cooked egg, creating a delicious and nutritious breakfast or brunch option.

NUTRITIVE VALUE PER WAFFLE:

- **Calories:** 321 kcal
- **Carbs:** 5g / **Sugars:** 3g / **Fibers:** 2g
- **Proteins:** 20g
- **Fats:** 26g
- **GI:** Low to Medium

HERE IS HOW TO MAKE IT:

01 Preheat your waffle iron according to the manufacturer's instructions.

02 In a large bowl, combine grated zucchini, almond or lentil flour, baking powder, and salt. Beat the eggs and add them to the zucchini mixture. Stir until well combined.

03 Lightly coat the waffle iron with cooking spray. Spoon the batter onto the hot waffle iron and spread it evenly. Close the iron and cook until golden and crispy.

04 While the waffles are cooking, fry or poach the eggs to your desired doneness.

05 Place a slice of crispy bacon on top of each cooked waffle, then top each with a fried or poached egg. Season with salt and pepper to taste.

PREP: 10 min   COOK: 20 min   SERVINGS: 4

INGREDIENTS YOU WILL NEED:

- 2 cups grated zucchini (GI: 15)
- 1/2 cup almond flour or lentil flour (GI: 10-25)
- 1/2 tsp baking powder
- 1/4 tsp salt
- 2 large eggs (GI: 0)
- Cooking spray
- 4 slices bacon, cooked until crispy (GI: 0)
- 4 large eggs, fried or poached (GI: 0)
- Salt and pepper to taste (GI: 0)

SERVING SUGGESTIONS:

- Serve with a small green salad.
- Drizzle with hot sauce or a dollop of Greek yogurt for extra flavor.
- These waffles can also be served with a classic egg salad or a tuna salad as an alternative to the egg and bacon topping.

PREP: 15 min   **COOK:** 20 min   **SERVINGS:** 4

PROTEIN-PACKED COTTAGE CHEESE BAGELS

These cottage cheese bagels made with low-carb flour are a delicious and healthy option for breakfast or a snack. Perfect for meal prepping, they can be stored in the refrigerator for up to a week or frozen for long-term storage. Customize with a variety of toppings for a satisfying and versatile meal.

HERE IS HOW TO MAKE IT:

01   **Prepare the dough:** preheat your oven to 350°F (175°C). Combine almond flour, cottage cheese, eggs, baking powder, and salt in a mixing bowl. Mix well until a dough forms.

02   **Shape the bagels:** divide the dough into 4 equal parts. Roll each part into a ball, then flatten slightly and use your finger to create a hole in the center to form a bagel shape.

03   **Add toppings:** sprinkle the tops with your choice of poppy seeds, sesame seeds, sunflower seeds, garlic powder, or onion flakes.

04   **Bake the Bagels:** place the bagels on a parchment-lined baking sheet. Brush the tops with olive oil. Bake for 20 minutes or until golden brown. Remove from the oven and let them cool on a wire rack.

INGREDIENTS YOU WILL NEED:

- 1 cup almond flour (GI: 25)
- 1 cup cottage cheese (GI: 30)
- 2 large eggs (GI: 0)
- 1 tsp baking powder (GI: 0)
- 1/4 tsp salt (GI: 0)
- 1 tbsp olive oil (GI: 0)
- **Optional toppings:** poppy seeds, sesame seeds, sunflower seeds, garlic powder, onion flakes

NUTRITIVE VALUE PER SERVING (1 BAGEL):

- **Calories:** 280 kcal
- **Carbs:** 5g / **Sugars:** 2g / **Fibers:** 3g
- **Proteins:** 14g
- **Fats:** 25g
- **GI:** Low

SERVING SUGGESTIONS:

Enjoy your bagels with the following topping variations:

01 With philadelphia cheese, smoked salmon, and cucumber:

- Spread Philadelphia cheese over the bagel.
- Top with slices of smoked salmon and cucumber.

02 With roasted red pepper and basil pesto:

- Spread basil pesto on the bagel.
- Add roasted red pepper strips.

03 With avocado, tomato, and sprouts:

- Mash avocado and spread on the bagel.
- Top with slices of tomato and fresh sprouts.

04 With mozzarella, sun-dried tomatoes, and basil:

- Place slices of mozzarella on the bagel.
- Top with sun-dried tomatoes and fresh basil leaves.

05 With hummus, sliced turkey and pickles:

- Spread hummus on bagel.
- Layer slices of turkey breast.
- Add thin slices of pickles.

06 With peanut butter and blueberries:

- Spread peanut butter on the bagel.
- Top with fresh blueberries.

PREP: 10 min   **COOK:** 15 min   **SERVINGS:** 2

WARM QUINOA BREAKFAST BOWL WITH BROCCOLI, SUNDRIED TOMATOES, AVOCADO & FETA

This hearty quinoa breakfast bowl combines warm quinoa with nutritious broccoli, tangy sundried tomatoes, creamy avocado, and salty feta cheese. It's a satisfying and wholesome option for a nutritious breakfast.

NUTRITIVE VALUE PER SERVING:

- **Calories:** 347 kcal
- **Carbs:** 29g / **Sugars:** 9g / **Fibers:** 9g
- **Proteins:** 10g
- **Fats:** 24g
- **GI:** Medium

INGREDIENTS YOU WILL NEED:

- 1/2 cup quinoa (GI: 53)
- 1 cup water
- 1 cup broccoli florets (GI: 15)
- 1/4 cup sundried tomatoes, chopped (GI: 30)
- 1 ripe avocado, diced (GI: 10)
- 1/4 cup crumbled feta cheese (GI: 30)
- 1 tbsp olive oil (GI: 0)
- Salt and pepper to taste (GI: 0)

SERVING SUGGESTIONS:

- Garnish with a poached or fried egg for added protein.

- Add a small handful of arugula for extra freshness and texture.

- True gourmets can elevate the dish with a few drops of truffle oil.

HERE IS HOW TO MAKE IT:

01 Rinse the quinoa thoroughly under cold water using a fine-mesh sieve.

02 In a small saucepan, bring the water to a boil. Add the rinsed quinoa and reduce heat to low. Cover and simmer for about 15 minutes or until the quinoa is tender and the water is absorbed. Fluff with a fork and set aside.

03 While the quinoa is cooking, steam or sauté the broccoli florets until tender-crisp, about 5-7 minutes.

04 In a large bowl, combine the cooked quinoa, chopped sundried tomatoes, and steamed broccoli. Toss gently to mix.

05 Divide the quinoa mixture between two bowls.

06 Top each bowl with diced avocado and crumbled feta cheese.

07 Drizzle with olive oil and season with salt and pepper to taste.

NUTRITIOUS GREEN BEAN AND PARMESAN OMELET

This omelet is a balanced, nutrient-dense option for breakfast or brunch. Packed with protein, healthy fats, and low-GI carbohydrates, it helps maintain stable blood sugar levels and keeps you feeling full for 4-5 hours.

NUTRITIVE VALUE PER SERVING:

- **Calories:** 232 kcal
- **Carbs:** 4g / **Sugars:** 2g / **Fibers:** 1g
- **Proteins:** 10g
- **Fats:** 14g
- **GI:** Low

HERE IS HOW TO MAKE IT:

01 Prepare the green beans: bring water to a boil in a small pot. Add the green beans and cook for 3-4 minutes until tender but still crisp. Drain and set aside.

02 Beat the eggs: in a bowl, beat the eggs until well combined. Season with salt and pepper.

03 Cook the omelet: in a non-stick skillet, heat the olive oil over medium heat. Add the beaten eggs and cook for 1-2 minutes until they start to set.

04 Add the fillings: sprinkle the cooked green beans and grated Parmesan evenly over one-half of the omelet. Cook for another 2-3 minutes until the eggs are fully set and the cheese is melted.

05 Fold and serve: fold the omelet in half and slide onto a plate. Serve immediately.

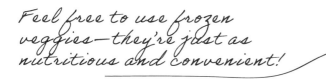

Feel free to use frozen veggies—they're just as nutritious and convenient!

PREP: 5 min   **COOK:** 10 min   **SERVINGS:** 1

INGREDIENTS YOU WILL NEED:

- 2 large eggs (GI: 0)
- ½ cup green beans, trimmed and chopped (GI: 15)
- ¼ cup grated Parmesan cheese (GI: 27)
- 1 tablespoon olive oil (GI: 0)
- Salt and pepper to taste (GI: 0)

SERVING SUGGESTIONS:

- Serve with a side of mixed greens or a simple tomato salad for a complete meal.
- Pair with whole grain toast or a small portion of quinoa for added fiber.
- Enjoy with a dollop of Greek yogurt or a sprinkle of fresh herbs like chives or parsley for extra flavor.

INGREDIENTS SWAPS AND SUBSTITUTIONS:

- **Eggs:** for a lower cholesterol option, use egg whites or a combination of whole eggs and egg whites.
- **Green beans:** Substitute with asparagus (GI: 15), spinach (GI: 15), mushrooms (GI: 10), or tomatoes (GI: 15) for a different flavor and texture.
- **Parmesan Cheese:** if needed, swap with feta (GI: 30), goat cheese (GI: 24), or a dairy-free alternative.

PREP: 10 min   COOK: 10 min   SERVINGS: 2

WHOLE GRAIN TOAST WITH TUNA & EGG SALAD

This veggie-loaded tuna salad, topped with creamy avocado and fresh sprouts, makes this toast a delicious and energizing option for busy mornings.

NUTRITIVE VALUE PER SERVING:

- **Calories:** 398 kcal
- **Carbs:** 22g / **Sugars:** 3.7g / **Fibers:** 8g
- **Proteins:** 36g
- **Fats:** 19g
- **GI:** Low

INGREDIENTS YOU WILL NEED:

- 2 slices whole grain bread (GI: 50)
- 1 can tuna, drained (GI: 0)
- 2 hard-boiled eggs, chopped (GI: 0)
- 1/4 cup celery, finely chopped (GI: 10)
- 1/4 cup Greek yogurt or mayonnaise (GI: 35-50)
- 1 tbsp Dijon mustard (GI: 35)
- 1 tbsp lemon juice (GI: 20)
- Salt and pepper, to taste (GI: 0)
- 1 avocado, sliced (GI: 10)
- 1/2 cup sprouts (such as alfalfa or radish) (GI: 0)

SERVING SUGGESTIONS:

- Pair with a side salad for a more substantial meal.

- You can add more flavor to your tuna salad by adding diced capers, dill pickles, or sweet relish.

- Adding lettuce, tomatoes, carrots and red onion gives you a boost of veggies that are packed with fiber and essential nutrients.

HERE IS HOW TO MAKE IT:

01 **Prepare the tuna salad:** in a mixing bowl, combine the drained tuna, chopped eggs, and celery. Add Greek yogurt (or mayonnaise), Dijon mustard, lemon juice, salt, and pepper. Mix until well combined.

02 **Toast the bread:** while preparing the tuna salad, toast the whole-grain bread slices to your desired level of crispiness.

03 **Assemble the toast:** spread the veggie-loaded tuna salad evenly over each slice of toasted bread.

04 **Top with avocado and sprouts:** Arrange avocado slices on top of the tuna salad and sprinkle with fresh sprouts.

STORAGE AND MEAL PREP:

Make the tuna salad ahead of time and store it in the refrigerator for up to 3 days. Assemble the toast fresh in the morning for a quick breakfast. The tuna salad can also be stored in an airtight container for easy transport.

CAULIFLOWER HASH BROWNS SERVED WITH GREEK YOGURT

These cauliflower hash browns are a delicious low-carb alternative to traditional hash browns. Served with creamy Greek yogurt, they make a satisfying and nutritious breakfast or snack.

NUTRITIVE VALUE PER SERVING:

- **Calories:** 237 kcal
- **Carbs:** 10.35g / **Sugars:** 5.21g / **Fibers:** 2.67g
- **Proteins:** 15.59g
- **Fats:** 14.24g
- **GI:** Low

HERE IS HOW TO MAKE IT:

01 Preheat your oven to 400°F (200°C).

02 Grate the cauliflower using a box grater or food processor until you have about 2 cups of grated cauliflower.

03 In a mixing bowl, combine the grated cauliflower, grated Parmesan cheese, beaten egg, garlic powder, salt, and pepper. Mix well until everything is thoroughly combined.

04 Line a baking sheet with parchment paper or lightly grease it with cooking spray or olive oil.

05 Take small portions of the cauliflower mixture and form them into hash brown patties, about 2-3 inches in diameter and 1/2 inch thick. Place them on the baking sheet.

06 Bake in the preheated oven for about 15-20 minutes, flipping halfway through, until the hash browns are golden brown and crispy on the outside.

07 Serve the cauliflower hash browns warm with a dollop of Greek yogurt on the side.

PREP: 15 min   **COOK:** 20 min   **SERVINGS:** 2

INGREDIENTS YOU WILL NEED:

- 1 small head of cauliflower, grated (GI: 15)
- 1/4 cup grated Parmesan cheese (GI: 27)
- 1 egg, beaten (GI: 0)
- 1/4 teaspoon garlic powder (GI: 0)
- Salt and pepper to taste (GI: 0)
- Cooking spray or olive oil (for greasing)

FOR SERVING:

- Greek yogurt (GI: 35)
- Fresh herbs (optional, for garnish)

SERVING SUGGESTIONS:

- Enjoy these cauliflower hash browns with a side of mixed greens or sliced tomatoes for a complete meal.
- They also pair well with avocado slices or a poached egg on top for added protein and flavor.

INGREDIENTS SWAPS AND SUBSTITUTIONS:

- Add diced bell peppers or onions to the cauliflower mixture for extra flavor and nutrients.

PREP: 10 min   **COOK:** 10 min   **SERVINGS:** 1

GREEK COTTAGE CHEESE BOWL

This savory cottage cheese bowl is a refreshing, protein-packed dish perfect for a healthy breakfast or light meal. It combines creamy cottage cheese with vibrant veggies, tangy olives, and crumbled feta for a satisfying Mediterranean-inspired flavor.

NUTRITIVE VALUE PER 3.5 OZ (100 GRAMS):

- **Calories:** 492 kcal
- **Carbs:** 20.94g / **Sugars:** 11.09g / **Fibers:** 3.96g
- **Proteins:** 28.45g
- **Fats:** 42.96g
- **GI:** Low

INGREDIENTS YOU WILL NEED:

- 1 cup cottage cheese (GI: 30)
- 1 tablespoon fresh dill, chopped (GI: 25)
- 4-5 cherry tomatoes (GI: 15)
- 1/4 yellow or orange bell pepper, diced (GI: 15)
- 2 mini cucumbers, sliced (GI: 15)
- Salt and pepper to season veggies (GI: 0)
- 4-5 pitted Kalamata olives, chopped (GI: 15)
- Salt and pepper to taste (GI: 0)
- 2 tablespoons crumbled feta cheese (GI: 30)
- Optional: Olive oil for drizzling

INGREDIENTS SWAPS AND SUBSTITUTIONS:

- Substitute fresh dill with basil or cilantro (coriander) for a different herb flavor.

- Substitute cherry tomatoes with sun-dried tomatoes for a richer taste.

- Replace Kalamata olives with capers for a salty twist.

HERE IS HOW TO MAKE IT:

01 In a bowl, combine the cottage cheese with chopped dill.

02 Arrange the cherry tomatoes, diced bell pepper, and sliced mini cucumbers on top of the cottage cheese.

03 Season with salt and pepper, if desired.

04 Sprinkle chopped olives and crumbled feta cheese over the veggies.

05 Optionally, drizzle with olive oil.

06 Serve immediately and enjoy!

Cottage cheese—a great protein source! Be sure to add it to your grocery list.

SCRAMBLED TOFU WITH SPINACH AND TOMATOES

This scrambled tofu with spinach and tomatoes is a nutritious and tasty breakfast inspired by Mediterranean flavors. Packed with plant-based protein, iron, calcium from spinach, and antioxidants from tomatoes, it offers a balanced and energizing start to your day, perfect for a low-GI meal.

NUTRITIVE VALUE PER SERVING:

- **Calories:** 188 kcal
- **Carbs:** 9.7g / **Sugars:** 3.8g / **Fibers:** 2.5g
- **Proteins:** 12g
- **Fats:** 13g
- **GI:** Low

PREP: 10 min   COOK: 10 min   SERVINGS: 2

HERE IS HOW TO MAKE IT:

01 Drain the tofu and crumble it into small pieces using your hands or a fork.

02 In a large skillet, heat the olive oil over medium heat. Add the chopped onion, minced garlic, and sauté until the onion becomes translucent, about 2-3 minutes.

03 Add the crumbled tofu to the skillet. Sprinkle with turmeric, paprika, salt, and pepper. Stir well to combine, cooking for about 5 minutes until the tofu is heated through and evenly coated with the spices.

04 Stir in the chopped spinach and halved cherry tomatoes. Cook for an additional 2-3 minutes until the spinach is wilted and the tomatoes are slightly softened.

05 Transfer the scrambled tofu to plates and serve immediately.

INGREDIENTS YOU WILL NEED:

- 1 block firm tofu, drained and crumbled (GI: 15)
- 1 cup fresh spinach, chopped (GI: 15)
- 1 cup cherry tomatoes, halved (GI: 15)
- 1 small onion, finely chopped (GI: 10)
- 2 garlic cloves, minced (GI: 35)
- 1 tbsp olive oil (GI: 0)
- 1/4 tsp turmeric powder (GI: 0)
- 1/4 tsp paprika (GI: 0)
- Salt and pepper to taste (GI: 0)

SERVING SUGGESTIONS:

- Serve with whole grain toast or a side of avocado slices for added fiber and healthy fats.
- Garnish with fresh herbs like cilantro or parsley for extra flavor.

INGREDIENTS SWAPS AND SUBSTITUTIONS:

- **Spinach:** substitute with kale or Swiss chard for a different leafy green option.

CHAPTER 10. FIBER-RICH START: SOUPS AND SALADS

As you already know, beginning meals with fiber-rich soups and salads not only tastes delicious but also significantly helps lower blood sugar levels. Research shows this approach can immediately reduce glucose spikes by 50% or more.

Imagine enjoying a hearty bowl of lentil soup or a fresh spinach salad before your main course—this simple step helps your body manage sugars more smoothly throughout the day. And, adding vinegar or lemon juice to salads or soups offers the additional benefit of lowering blood glucose levels. It's truly a win-win for both your health and taste buds!

Numerous studies have shown that vinegar (acetic acid) can help prevent blood sugar spikes in people with prediabetes and type 2 diabetes by blocking starch absorption. This helps maintain balanced blood sugar levels and indirectly prevents weight gain. Some research has also indicated that vinegar regulates insulin release.
In this chapter, you'll discover a delightful variety of salad and soup recipes from around the world. Each recipe is crafted to be both flavorful and supportive of your health goals.

TOM YUM SOUP WITH ZUCCHINI NOODLES

This light and refreshing soup is inspired by Thai cuisine, with aromatic herbs and spices. It's packed with vibrant flavors from nutritious vegetables, making it a perfect choice for a delicious, low-calorie meal.

NUTRITIVE VALUE PER SERVING:

- **Calories:** 168 kcal
- **Carbs:** 18.61g / **Sugars:** 9.42g / **Fibers:** 3.94g
- **Proteins:** 14.70g
- **Fats:** 5.97g
- **GI:** Low

HERE IS HOW TO MAKE IT:

01 In a large pot, bring the vegetable broth to a boil. Add lemongrass, ginger (or galangal), and Thai red chilies. Reduce heat to medium-low and simmer for 5-7 minutes to infuse flavors.

02 Add tofu cubes and simmer for another 5 minutes until tofu is heated through and infused with the soup flavors.

03 Stir in zucchini noodles, tomato wedges, onion slices, and mushrooms. Cook for 3-4 minutes until vegetables are tender yet still crisp.

04 Remove the soup from heat. Stir in fresh cilantro, lime juice, and soy sauce or tamari. Adjust seasoning with salt to taste.

05 Divide the Tom Yum Soup with Zucchini Noodles into bowls and serve hot.

INGREDIENTS SWAPS AND SUBSTITUTIONS:

- **Kaffir lime leaves:** If not available, substitute with additional lime zest or a small amount of lime juice for citrusy flavor.

- **Galangal:** Substitute with fresh ginger, though galangal has a more citrusy and peppery flavor.

PREP: 15 min   **COOK:** 15 min   **SERVINGS:** 2

INGREDIENTS YOU WILL NEED:

- 4 cups vegetable broth

- 1 stalk lemongrass, smashed and cut into pieces (GI: 0)

- 2-3 slices ginger (or galangal if available) (GI: 0)

- 2-3 Thai red chilies, sliced (adjust to taste) (GI: 0)

- 200g firm tofu, cut into cubes (GI: 15)

- 1 medium zucchini, spiralized into noodles (GI: 15)

- 1 tomato, cut into wedges (GI: 15))

- 1 small onion, thinly sliced (GI: 10)

- 1/2 cup mushrooms, sliced (GI: 10)

- 1/4 cup fresh cilantro leaves (GI: 15)

- 2 tbsp lime juice (GI: 20)

- 1 tbsp soy sauce or tamari (GI: 20)

- Salt to taste (GI: 0)

SERVING SUGGESTIONS:

- Garnish with extra cilantro leaves and a lime wedge for additional freshness.

- Serve as a light main dish, and consider adding boiled egg, shrimp, or chicken for additional protein.

PREP: 15 min   COOK: 40 min   SERVINGS: 4

SOUP WITH PORCINI MUSHROOMS AND PEARL BARLEY

This savory cottage cheese bowl is a refreshing, protein-packed dish perfect for a healthy breakfast or light meal. It combines creamy cottage cheese with vibrant veggies, tangy olives, and crumbled feta for a satisfying Mediterranean-inspired flavor.

NUTRITIVE VALUE PER PER SERVING (APPROXIMATE):

- **Calories:** 108 kcal
- **Carbs:** 22g / **Sugars:** 5g / **Fibers:** 10g
- **Proteins:** 8g
- **Fats:** 1g
- **GI:** Low

INGREDIENTS YOU WILL NEED:

- 1 cup pearl barley (GI: 25)
- 1 ounce dried porcini mushrooms (or 8 ounces fresh/frozen porcini mushrooms) (GI: 0)
- 1 onion, finely chopped (GI: 10)
- 2 carrots, diced (GI: 35)
- 2 celery stalks, diced (GI: 15)
- 2 cloves garlic, minced (GI: 35)
- 6 cups vegetable broth (GI: 0)
- 1 bay leaf
- Salt and pepper to taste (GI: 0)
- Fresh parsley or thyme for garnish (optional)

INGREDIENTS SWAPS AND SUBSTITUTIONS:

- Substitute vegetable broth with mushroom or chicken broth for a different flavor profile.
- Use other types of mushrooms, such as button mushrooms or cremini mushrooms, if porcini mushrooms are not available.

HERE IS HOW TO MAKE IT:

01 If using dried porcini mushrooms, soak them in hot water for about 20 minutes until they are softened. Drain and chop them into smaller pieces.

02 In a large pot, heat olive oil over medium heat. Add the chopped onion, carrots, and celery. Sauté for 5-7 minutes until the vegetables begin to soften.

03 Add minced garlic and cook for another 1-2 minutes until fragrant.

04 Stir in the pearl barley and chopped porcini mushrooms. Cook for 1-2 minutes, stirring occasionally.

05 Pour in the vegetable broth and add the bay leaf. Bring the mixture to a boil, then reduce the heat to low. Cover and simmer for about 30 minutes, or until the barley is tender.

06 Season with salt and pepper to taste. Remove the bay leaf before serving.

07 Ladle the soup into bowls. Garnish with fresh parsley or thyme if desired. Serve hot, accompanied by crusty bread.

TOMATO SEAFOOD SOUP

Inspired by the vibrant flavors of Mediterranean cuisine, this delicious soup combines fresh seafood with a rich tomato broth, capturing the essence of seaside cooking. It's a beloved dish in coastal towns, known for being both light and flavorful.

NUTRITIVE VALUE PER SERVING (APPROXIMATE):

- **Calories:** 200 kcal
- **Carbs:** 12g / **Sugars:** 6g / **Fibers:** 3g
- **Proteins:** 20g
- **Fats:** 8g
- **GI:** Low

HERE IS HOW TO MAKE IT:

01 In a large pot, heat olive oil over medium heat. Add the chopped onion, carrot, and celery. Sauté for 5-7 minutes until the vegetables begin to soften.

02 Add minced garlic and cook for another 1-2 minutes until fragrant.

03 Stir in the diced tomatoes and tomato paste. Cook for another 5 minutes, stirring occasionally.

04 Pour in the seafood or fish broth and white wine (if using). Add the dried oregano, dried basil, bay leaf, and red pepper flakes (if using). Bring the mixture to a boil, then reduce the heat to low. Cover and simmer for about 15 minutes.

05 Add the mixed seafood to the pot. Continue to simmer for another 10 minutes, or until the seafood is cooked through and tender.

06 Stir in the chopped parsley and season with salt and pepper to taste.

07 Just before serving, add 1 lemon juice and stir well.

08 Ladle the soup into bowls. Garnish with additional fresh parsley if desired. Serve hot.

PREP: 20 min **COOK:** 30 min **SERVINGS:** 6

INGREDIENTS YOU WILL NEED:

- 2 tbsp olive oil (GI: 0)
- 1 onion, finely chopped (GI: 10)
- 2 garlic cloves, minced (GI: 35)
- 1 carrot, diced (GI: 35)
- 2 celery stalks, diced (GI: 15)
- 1 can (14.5 ounces) diced tomatoes (GI: 15)
- 1/4 cup tomato paste (GI: 45)
- 4 cups seafood or fish broth (GI: 0)
- 1/2 cup dry white wine (optional) (GI: 30-40)
- 1 tsp dried oregano (GI: 0)
- 1 tsp dried basil (GI: 0)
- 1 bay leaf (GI: 0)
- 1/2 tsp red pepper flakes (optional) (GI: 0)
- 1 pound mixed seafood (shrimp, scallops, squid, and/or white fish), cleaned and cut into bite-sized pieces (GI: 0)
- 1/2 cup fresh parsley, chopped (GI: 15)
- Salt and pepper to taste (GI: 0)
- Juice of 1 lemon (GI: 20)

INGREDIENTS SWAPS AND SUBSTITUTIONS:

- Substitute mixed seafood with just shrimp or just fish if preferred.

- Use fresh tomatoes instead of canned for a lighter, fresher flavor.

PREP: 15 min   **COOK:** 45 min   **SERVINGS:** 4

SPICY CHICKEN BREAST AND RED LENTIL SOUP

This Spicy Chicken Breast and Red Lentil Soup is a hearty dish with a touch of Indian-inspired flavors. Packed with protein-rich chicken and low-GI red lentils, it's both satisfying and nutritious, ideal for a comforting meal.

NUTRITIVE VALUE PER PER SERVING (APPROXIMATE):

- **Calories:** 282 kcal
- **Carbs:** 23g / **Sugars:** 5g / **Fibers:** 17g
- **Proteins:** 29g
- **Fats:** 3g
- **GI:** Low

INGREDIENTS YOU WILL NEED:

- 1 cup dried red lentils (GI: 21)
- 2 boneless, skinless chicken breasts, diced (GI: 0)
- 1 onion, finely chopped (GI: 10)
- 2 carrots, diced (GI: 35)
- 2 celery stalks, diced (GI: 15)
- 2 cloves garlic, minced (GI: 35)
- 1-inch piece of ginger, minced (GI: 0)
- 1 tsp ground cumin (GI: 0)
- 1 tsp ground coriander (GI: 0)
- 1/2 tsp turmeric powder (GI: 0)
- 1/4 tsp paprika (adjust to taste) (GI: 0)
- 6 cups chicken broth (GI: 0)
- Salt and pepper to taste (GI: 0)
- Fresh cilantro for garnish (optional)

SERVING SUGGESTIONS:

- Add a dollop of Greek yogurt or a squeeze of fresh lime juice for extra flavor.

INGREDIENTS SWAPS AND SUBSTITUTIONS:

- Use green lentils or another variety of lentils if red lentils are not available.
- Substitute chicken broth with vegetable broth for a vegetarian option.

HERE IS HOW TO MAKE IT:

01 Rinse the red lentils under cold water and drain.

02 In a large pot, heat olive oil over medium heat. Add the chopped onion, carrots, and celery. Sauté for 5-7 minutes until the vegetables begin to soften.

03 Add minced garlic and cook for another 1-2 minutes until fragrant.

04 Stir in the ground cumin, coriander, turmeric powder, and paprika. Cook for 1 minute to toast the spices.

05 Add the diced chicken breasts and red lentils to the pot. Pour in the chicken broth and bring the mixture to a boil.

06 Reduce the heat to low, cover, and simmer for about 30-35 minutes, or until the lentils are tender and the chicken is cooked through.

07 Season with salt and pepper to taste.

08 Ladle the soup into bowls. Garnish with fresh cilantro if desired. Serve hot.

AVOCADO, MANGO SALAD WITH ARUGULA AND PINE NUTS

A refreshing salad combining creamy avocado, sweet mango for Asian-inspired notes, peppery arugula, and crunchy pine nuts, dressed with a tangy vinaigrette.

NUTRITIVE VALUE PER SERVING:

- **Calories:** 290 kcal
- **Carbs:** 20g / **Sugars:** 12g / **Fibers:** 7g
- **Proteins:** 4g
- **Fats:** 15g
- **GI:** Low

HERE IS HOW TO MAKE IT:

01 **Prepare the dressing:** in a small bowl, whisk together olive oil, lemon juice, salt, and pepper.

02 **Assemble the salad:** in a large salad bowl, combine diced avocado, diced mango, arugula, and toasted pine nuts.

03 **Add the dressing:** drizzle the dressing over the salad ingredients and gently toss to coat evenly.

INGREDIENTS SWAPS AND SUBSTITUTIONS:

- Substitute arugula with baby spinach or mixed greens.
- Replace pine nuts with almonds, walnuts, or pumpkin seeds for variety.

PREP: 15 min   COOK: N/A   SERVINGS: 4

INGREDIENTS YOU WILL NEED:

- 2 ripe avocados, peeled, pitted, and diced (GI: 15)
- 1 large mango, peeled, pitted, and diced (GI: 56)
- 4 cups arugula (GI: 10)
- 1/4 cup pine nuts, toasted (GI: 15)
- 1/4 cup extra virgin olive oil (GI: 0)
- 2 tablespoons lemon juice (GI: 20)
- Salt and pepper to taste

SERVING SUGGESTIONS:

- Enjoy as a light lunch or serve alongside grilled chicken or fish for a complete meal.

Arugula, known as the "queen of detox," stimulates bile flow and is rich in antioxidants and vitamins

PREP: 20 min   **COOK:** 15 min   **SERVINGS:** 4

QUINOA & VEGGIE SALAD WITH ZESTY TAHINI LEMON DRESSING

This vibrant salad captures the essence of freshness with a blend of quinoa, colorful vegetables, and a zesty tahini lemon dressing. It's a nutritious and satisfying dish perfect for any meal, offering a delightful mix of flavors and textures.

NUTRITIVE VALUE PER SERVING (APPROXIMATE):

- **Calories:** 235 kcal
- **Carbs:** 35g / **Sugars:** 6g / **Fibers:** 5g
- **Proteins:** 8g
- **Fats:** 10g
- **GI:** Low

INGREDIENTS YOU WILL NEED:

- 1 cup quinoa, rinsed (GI: 35-40)
- 2 cups water
- 1 cup cherry tomatoes, halved (GI: 15)
- 1 cucumber, diced (GI: 15)
- 1 red bell pepper, diced (GI: 15)
- 1/2 red onion, finely chopped (GI: 10)
- 1/4 cup fresh parsley, chopped (GI: 15)
- 1/4 cup fresh mint, chopped (GI: 5)

ZESTY TAHINI LEMON DRESSING:

- 1/4 cup tahini (GI: 40)
- Juice of 1 lemon (GI: 20)
- 2 tbsp olive oil (GI: 0)
- 2 tbsp water (adjust for desired consistency)
- 1 garlic clove, minced (GI: 30)
- 1 tsp ground cumin
- Salt and pepper to taste

INGREDIENTS SWAPS AND SUBSTITUTIONS:

- Add other fresh vegetables like shredded carrots, radishes, or avocado for extra color and nutrients.

HERE IS HOW TO MAKE IT:

01 Combine quinoa and water in a medium saucepan. Bring to a boil, then simmer on low, covered, for about 15 minutes until quinoa is tender and water is absorbed. Remove from heat and cool.

02 Prepare the vegetables. Halve the cherry tomatoes, dice the cucumber and red bell pepper, finely chop the red onion, and chop the parsley and mint.

03 In a large bowl, combine the cooled quinoa with the prepared vegetables and herbs. Mix well.

04 To make the dressing, whisk together the tahini, lemon juice, olive oil, water, minced garlic, ground cumin, salt, and pepper in a small bowl until smooth and creamy.

05 Pour the dressing over the quinoa and veggie mixture. Toss well to coat all the ingredients evenly with the dressing.

06 Adjust the seasoning with additional salt and pepper if needed.

07 Serve the salad immediately, or chill it in the refrigerator for 30 minutes to let the flavors meld.

GREEK AVOCADO & CHICKEN SALAD

A refreshing and nutritious salad inspired by Mediterranean flavors, featuring grilled chicken, creamy avocado, and tangy feta cheese, all complemented by a zesty lemon dressing.

NUTRITIVE VALUE PER SERVING (APPROXIMATE):

- **Calories:** 203 kcal
- **Carbs:** 12g / **Sugars:** 6g / **Fibers:** 3g
- **Proteins:** 20g
- **Fats:** 8g
- **GI:** Low

HERE IS HOW TO MAKE IT:

01 Grill the chicken breasts until cooked through, then slice them thinly.

02 In a large bowl, combine the grilled chicken slices, diced avocado, cherry tomatoes, cucumber, red onion, Kalamata olives, and crumbled feta cheese.

03 In a small bowl, whisk together extra virgin olive oil, lemon juice, minced garlic, dried oregano, salt, and pepper.

04 Pour the dressing over the salad ingredients and gently toss to coat evenly. Adjust seasoning with salt and pepper if needed.

INGREDIENTS SWAPS AND SUBSTITUTIONS:

- Substitute grilled chicken with grilled shrimp for a seafood twist.

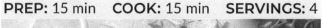

PREP: 15 min   **COOK:** 15 min   **SERVINGS:** 4

INGREDIENTS YOU WILL NEED:

- 2 boneless, skinless chicken breasts, grilled and sliced (GI: 0)
- 1 large avocado, diced (GI: 15)
- 1 cup cherry tomatoes, halved (GI: 30)
- 1/2 cucumber, diced (GI: 15)
- 1/4 red onion, thinly sliced (GI: 15)
- 1/4 cup Kalamata olives, pitted and halved (GI: 15)
- 1/4 cup crumbled feta cheese (GI: 30)
- Fresh parsley or dill, chopped (for garnish)
- Salt and pepper to taste

SERVING SUGGESTIONS:

- Serve the salad as a light main dish or as a side with crusty bread.
- Garnish with chopped fresh parsley or dill for added freshness.

This salad is a great option for a full lunch or dinner, and also perfect for meal prep. It's nutritious, filling, and never gets boring. An excellent solution when you don't know what to cook.

PREP: 15 min   **COOK:** 20 min   **SERVINGS:** 4

STRAWBERRY, AVOCADO, QUINOA, AND SPINACH SALAD WITH PECAN BRITTLE

This vibrant salad combines fresh strawberries, creamy avocado, hearty quinoa, and nutritious spinach. It is topped with crunchy pecan brittle for added texture and flavor.

NUTRITIVE VALUE PER SERVING (APPROXIMATE):

- **Calories:** 345 kcal
- **Carbs:** 35g / **Sugars:** 7g / **Fibers:** 7g
- **Proteins:** 7g
- **Fats:** 10g
- **GI:** Low

INGREDIENTS YOU WILL NEED:

- 1 cup quinoa, rinsed (GI: 35-40)
- 2 cups water
- 2 cups fresh spinach leaves, chopped (GI: 15)
- 1 cup strawberries, sliced (GI: 40)
- 1 ripe avocado, diced (GI: 15)
- 1/4 cup pecans, chopped (GI: 10)
- 1/4 cup extra virgin olive oil (GI: 0)
- 2 tablespoons lemon juice (GI: 20)
- Salt and pepper to taste
- Balsamic glaze (optional)

SERVING SUGGESTIONS:

- Enjoy as a light lunch or serve alongside grilled chicken or fish for a complete meal.

INGREDIENTS SWAPS AND SUBSTITUTIONS:

- Substitute pecans with walnuts or almonds.
- Replace strawberries with raspberries or blueberries for variation.

HERE IS HOW TO MAKE IT:

01 Combine quinoa and water in a medium saucepan. Bring to a boil, then simmer on low, covered, for about 15 minutes until quinoa is tender and water is absorbed. Remove from heat and cool.

02 In a small skillet, toast chopped pecans over medium heat until fragrant, about 3-5 minutes. Remove from heat and spread onto parchment paper to cool and harden.

03 In a large salad bowl, combine cooked quinoa, chopped spinach, sliced strawberries, diced avocado, and toastedpecan brittle.

04 Drizzle the dressing over the salad ingredients and gently toss to coat evenly. Optionally, garnish with additional pecan brittle or a drizzle of balsamic glaze.

ROASTED BEET SALAD WITH ORANGE, GOAT CHEESE, ARUGULA AND CREAMY MUSTARD DRESSING

A vibrant salad bursting with earthy roasted beets, sweet citrusy oranges, creamy goat cheese, peppery arugula, and a touch of tangy mustard dressing.

NUTRITIVE VALUE PER SERVING (APPROXIMATE):

- **Calories:** 280 kcal
- **Carbs:** 25g / **Sugars:** 15g / **Fibers:** 5g
- **Proteins:** 6g
- **Fats:** 12g
- **GI:** Low

HERE IS HOW TO MAKE IT:

01 Wash beets thoroughly, trim tops, drizzle with olive oil and wrap in foil. Roast at 400°F (200°C) for 45 minutes, or until tender. Peel and dice when cool enough to handle.

02 In a small bowl, whisk together olive oil, Dijon mustard, apple cider vinegar, lemon juice, salt and pepper until smooth.

03 In a large salad bowl, combine diced beets, orange segments, arugula, and crumbled goat cheese.

04 Drizzle the creamy mustard dressing over the salad ingredients and gently toss to coat evenly.

05 Sprinkle with toasted walnuts for added crunch.

INGREDIENTS SWAPS AND SUBSTITUTIONS:

- Substitute walnuts with pecans, pistachios, or sunflower seeds.
- If goat cheese is not your preference, crumbled feta or blue cheese can be used instead.

PREP: 15 min   **COOK:** 45 min   **SERVINGS:** 4

INGREDIENTS YOU WILL NEED:

- 2 medium beets, roasted and diced (about 2 cups) (GI: 55)
- 1 large orange, peeled and segmented (GI: 35)
- 4 cups arugula (GI: 15)
- 4 ounces goat cheese, crumbled (GI: 20)
- 1/4 cup walnuts, toasted (optional) (GI: 15)

CREAMY MUSTARD DRESSING:

- 1/4 cup olive oil (GI: 0)
- 2 tablespoons Dijon mustard (GI: 35)
- 1 tablespoon apple cider vinegar (GI: 15)
- 1 tablespoon lemon juice (GI: 20)
- Salt and pepper to taste

TIPS:

Roasting and then cooling starchy vegetables (like beets) before consumption lowers their glycemic index compared to boiling while also preserving a more intense flavor.

PREP: 20 min   **COOK:** 15 min   **SERVINGS:** 4

LEMON SHRIMP, AVOCADO, AND TOMATO SALAD

This vibrant and refreshing salad combines lemon-marinated shrimp with creamy avocado, juicy tomatoes, and mixed greens. Topped with a poached egg and crunchy pumpkin seeds, it's a nutritious and satisfying dish perfect for a light meal.

NUTRITIVE VALUE PER SERVING (APPROXIMATE):

- **Calories:** 350 kcal
- **Carbs:** 10g / **Sugars:** 3g / **Fibers:** 5g
- **Proteins:** 20g
- **Fats:** 20g
- **GI:** Low

INGREDIENTS YOU WILL NEED:

- 1 lb shrimp, peeled and deveined (GI: 0)
- 1 large avocado, diced (GI: 15)
- 1 cup cherry tomatoes, halved (GI: 15)
- 4 cups mixed salad greens (GI: 5)
- 4 large eggs (GI: 0)
- 1/4 cup pumpkin seeds, toasted (GI: 10)
- 2 tablespoons fresh lemon juice (GI: 20)
- 2 tablespoons olive oil (GI: 0)
- 1 garlic clove, minced (GI: 30)
- Salt and pepper to taste (GI: 0)

SERVING SUGGESTIONS:

- Serve immediately to enjoy the contrast of warm shrimp and poached egg with the cool salad.

INGREDIENTS SWAPS AND SUBSTITUTIONS:

- Substitute shrimp with grilled chicken or tofu for a different protein source.

HERE IS HOW TO MAKE IT:

01 In a bowl, combine the shrimp with 1 tablespoon of lemon juice, 1 tablespoon of olive oil, minced garlic, salt, and pepper. Let it marinate for 10 minutes.

02 In a large skillet over medium heat, cook the marinated shrimp for about 2-3 minutes per side or until they turn pink and opaque. Remove from heat and let them cool slightly.

03 Bring a pot of water to a gentle simmer. Crack an egg into a small bowl, then gently slide it into the simmering water. Cook for 3-4 minutes until the white is set but the yolk is still runny. Remove with a slotted spoon and repeat with the remaining eggs.

04 In a large bowl, combine the mixed salad greens, diced avocado, cherry tomatoes and cooked shrimp.

05 In a small bowl, whisk together the remaining lemon juice and olive oil. Season with salt and pepper to taste. Pour the dressing over the salad and toss gently to combine.

06 Divide the salad among four plates. Top each with a poached egg and sprinkle with toasted pumpkin seeds.

ASPARAGUS, TOMATO SALAD WITH BURRATA CHEESE, PINE-NUTS & BALSAMIC DRESSING

This elegant and flavorful salad features tender asparagus, juicy tomatoes, and creamy burrata cheese, complemented by the crunch of pine nuts and a tangy balsamic dressing. It's a perfect dish for any occasion, showcasing the best of fresh, seasonal ingredients.

PREP: 15 min   **COOK:** 10 min   **SERVINGS:** 4

NUTRITIVE VALUE PER SERVING (APPROXIMATE):

- **Calories:** 280 kcal
- **Carbs:** 12g / **Sugars:** 5g / **Fibers:** 4g
- **Proteins:** 12g
- **Fats:** 20g
- **GI:** Low

HERE IS HOW TO MAKE IT:

01 Bring a pot of water to a boil. Add the trimmed asparagus and cook for 2-3 minutes until bright green and tender-crisp. Drain and immediately plunge into ice water to stop the cooking process. Drain again and set aside.

02 In a small bowl, whisk together the balsamic vinegar, olive oil, and minced garlic. Season with salt and pepper to taste.

03 On a large serving platter, arrange the blanched asparagus and halved cherry tomatoes. Tear the burrata cheese into pieces and scatter over the vegetables.

04 Drizzle the balsamic dressing evenly over the salad. Sprinkle the toasted pine nuts and chopped basil leaves over the top.

INGREDIENTS YOU WILL NEED:

- 1 bunch asparagus, trimmed and blanched (GI: 15)
- 2 cups cherry tomatoes, halved (GI: 15)
- 1 ball burrata cheese (GI: 25)
- 1/4 cup pine nuts, toasted (GI: 10)
- 2 tablespoons balsamic vinegar (GI: 15)
- 2 tablespoons olive oil (GI: 0)
- 1 garlic clove, minced (GI: 35)
- Fresh basil leaves, chopped (GI: 5)
- Salt and pepper to taste (GI: 0)

INGREDIENTS SWAPS AND SUBSTITUTIONS:

- Substitute pine nuts with slivered almonds or chopped walnuts for a different nutty flavor.
- Use mozzarella or goat cheese instead of burrata for a variation in cheese texture and taste.

Asparagus is a fantastic seasonal veggie that's great in many dishes, like sides and salads. It's perfect for weight management—low in calories and high in fiber! Plus, it helps with digestion.

PREP: 15 min **COOK:** 30 min **SERVINGS:** 4

MIDDLE EASTERN ROASTED EGGPLANT SALAD WITH TAHINI DRESSING

This delightful salad hails from the rich culinary traditions of the Middle East, where eggplants are a staple ingredient. The combination of roasted eggplant and creamy tahini dressing creates a harmonious blend of smoky and nutty flavors, making it a perfect dish for a refreshing and satisfying meal.

NUTRITIVE VALUE PER SERVING (APPROXIMATE):

- **Calories:** 290 kcal
- **Carbs:** 18g / **Sugars:** 7g / **Fibers:** 8g
- **Proteins:** 6g
- **Fats:** 14g
- **GI:** Low

INGREDIENTS YOU WILL NEED:

- 2 medium eggplants, diced (GI: 15)
- 2 tablespoons olive oil (GI: 0)
- 1 cup cherry tomatoes, halved (GI: 15)
- 1/2 red onion, thinly sliced (GI: 10)
- 1/4 cup fresh parsley, chopped (GI: 15)
- 1/4 cup fresh mint, chopped (GI: 5)
- 1/4 cup pomegranate seeds (GI: 35)
- 1/4 cup toasted pine nuts (GI: 15)

FOR THE TAHINI DRESSING:

- 1/4 cup tahini (GI: 40)
- 2 tablespoons lemon juice (GI: 20)
- 1 garlic clove, minced (GI: 35)
- 2 tablespoons water (GI: 0)
- Salt and pepper to taste (GI: 0)

SERVING SUGGESTIONS:

- Serve as a light main dish or as a side to grilled meats or fish.
- Garnish with extra pomegranate seeds and a sprinkle of fresh herbs for added color and flavor.

HERE IS HOW TO MAKE IT:

01 Preheat your oven to 400°F (200°C).

02 Toss the diced eggplant with olive oil and spread it out on a baking sheet. Roast for 25-30 minutes, or until the eggplant is tender and slightly caramelized.

03 While the eggplant is roasting, prepare the tahini dressing. In a small bowl, whisk together the tahini, lemon juice, minced garlic, water, salt, and pepper until smooth.

04 In a large bowl, combine the roasted eggplant, cherry tomatoes, red onion, parsley, mint, pomegranate seeds, and toasted pine nuts.

05 Drizzle the tahini dressing over the salad and toss gently to combine.

06 Serve the salad immediately or let it chill in the refrigerator for 30 minutes to allow the flavors to meld.

MEDITERRANEAN CHICKPEA, TUNA SALAD WITH FETA & LEMONY DRESSING

Inspired by the healthy Mediterranean diet, this salad is packed with protein and fiber, making it a perfect light meal or side dish.

NUTRITIVE VALUE PER SERVING (APPROXIMATE):

- **Calories:** 320 kcal
- **Carbs:** 22g / **Sugars:** 4g / **Fibers:** 7g
- **Proteins:** 20g
- **Fats:** 15g
- **GI:** Low

PREP: 15 min   **COOK:** 0 min   **SERVINGS:** 4

HERE IS HOW TO MAKE IT:

01 In a large salad bowl, combine the chickpeas, tuna, mixed salad greens, cucumber, roasted red bell pepper, red onion, and Kalamata olives.

02 In a small bowl, whisk together the olive oil, fresh lemon juice, minced garlic, Dijon mustard, salt, and pepper until well combined.

03 Pour the dressing over the salad and toss gently to coat all the ingredients evenly.

04 Sprinkle the crumbled feta cheese and chopped parsley over the top of the salad. Serve immediately and enjoy!

INGREDIENTS SWAPS AND SUBSTITUTIONS:

- Replace tuna with grilled chicken or turkey breast for a different protein option.

- Use cherry tomatoes instead of roasted red bell pepper for a fresh twist.

- Swap feta cheese with goat cheese for a creamier texture.

INGREDIENTS YOU WILL NEED:

- 1 can (15 oz) chickpeas, drained and rinsed (GI: 28)
- 2 cans (5 oz each) tuna in water, drained (GI: 0)
- 4 cups mixed salad greens (GI: Low)
- 1 cucumber, diced (GI: 15)
- 1 cup roasted red bell pepper, sliced (GI: 15)
- 1/2 red onion, thinly sliced (GI: 10)
- 1/2 cup Kalamata olives, pitted and halved (GI: 15)
- 1/2 cup crumbled feta cheese (GI: 30)
- Fresh parsley, chopped (for garnish)

FOR THE LEMONY DRESSING:

- 1/4 cup extra virgin olive oil (GI: 0)
- 2 tbsp fresh lemon juice (GI: 20)
- 1 garlic clove, minced (GI: 35)
- 1 tsp Dijon mustard (GI: 35)
- Salt and pepper to taste (GI: 0)

PREP: 20 min   **COOK:** 10 min   **SERVINGS:** 4

THAI BEEF SALAD WITH FIERY CHILI DRESSING

Inspired by the vibrant flavors of Thai cuisine, this salad is perfect for a light yet satisfying meal.

NUTRITIVE VALUE PER SERVING (APPROXIMATE):

- **Calories:** 370 kcal
- **Carbs:** 32g / **Sugars:** 6g / **Fibers:** 4g
- **Proteins:** 22g
- **Fats:** 12g
- **GI:** Medium

HERE IS HOW TO MAKE IT:

01   Cook the glass noodles according to package instructions. Drain and set aside.

02   In a large skillet, heat the olive oil over medium-high heat. Add the sliced beef and cook for 3-5 minutes until browned and cooked to your liking. Remove from heat and let it cool slightly.

03   In a small bowl, whisk together the lime juice, fish sauce, soy sauce, olive oil, minced garlic, chopped red chili, sugar substitute, salt, and pepper.

04   In a large mixing bowl, combine the cooked glass noodles, cherry tomatoes, cucumber, red bell pepper, red onion, cilantro, and mint. Add the cooked beef.

05   Pour the lime dressing over the salad and toss gently to combine, ensuring all ingredients are evenly coated.Sprinkle with chopped peanuts, and serve immediately.

INGREDIENTS YOU WILL NEED:

- 1 lb beef sirloin, thinly sliced (GI: 0)
- 1 tablespoon olive oil (GI: 0)
- 200g glass noodles (GI: 45)
- 1 cup cherry tomatoes, halved (GI: 15)
- 1 cucumber, thinly sliced (GI: 10)
- 1 red bell pepper, thinly sliced (GI: 15)
- 1/4 red onion, thinly sliced (GI: 10)
- 1 cup fresh cilantro, chopped (GI: 15)
- 1 cup fresh mint leaves, chopped (GI: 5)
- 1/4 cup chopped peanuts (GI: 14)

FOR THE LIME DRESSING:

- 1/4 cup fresh lime juice (GI: 20)
- 2 tablespoons fish sauce (GI: 0)
- 1 tablespoon soy sauce (GI: 20)
- 1 tablespoon olive oil (GI: 0)
- 1 garlic clove, minced (GI: 35)
- 1 red chili, finely chopped (GI: 0)
- Sugar substitute to taste (GI: 0)
- Salt and pepper to taste (GI: 0)

INGREDIENTS SWAPS AND SUBSTITUTIONS:

- **Beef:** Substitute with turkey breast or grilled chicken for a lighter option.
- **Glass noodles:** Use rice noodles or whole wheat noodles as an alternative.
- **Peanuts:** Swap with cashews or almonds for a different nutty flavor.

SERVING SUGGESTIONS:

- Serve as a main dish for a light lunch or dinner.
- Pair with a side of fresh summer rolls for a complete Thai-inspired meal.

ASIAN CABBAGE SALAD WITH EDAMAME, ALMOND FLAKES, AND GINGER PEANUT DRESSING

This Asian-inspired cabbage salad is a delightful mix of crunchy vegetables, protein-packed edamame, and nutty almond flakes, all tossed in a flavorful ginger peanut dressing. It's a vibrant, nutritious dish perfect for any meal.

NUTRITIVE VALUE PER SERVING (APPROXIMATE):

- **Calories:** 275 kcal
- **Carbs:** 24g / **Sugars:** 7g / **Fibers:** 6g
- **Proteins:** 10g
- **Fats:** 12g
- **GI:** Low

HERE IS HOW TO MAKE IT:

01 In a large salad bowl, combine the shredded cabbage, sliced red bell pepper, julienned carrot, cooked edamame, toasted almond flakes, and sliced green onions.

02 In a small bowl, whisk together the peanut butter, rice vinegar, soy sauce, sesame oil, minced garlic, and grated ginger until smooth. Add water as needed to achieve desired consistency.

03 Pour the ginger peanut dressing over the salad and toss well to coat all the ingredients evenly.

04 Garnish with chopped fresh cilantro.

SERVING SUGGESTIONS:

- Serve as a side dish to grilled chicken or tofu for a complete meal.

- Top with grilled shrimp or beef strips for added protein.

PREP: 20 min   COOK: 0 min   SERVINGS: 4

INGREDIENTS YOU WILL NEED:

- 4 cups shredded green cabbage (GI: 10)
- 1 red bell pepper, thinly sliced (GI: 15)
- 1 large carrot, julienned (GI: 35)
- 1 cup shelled edamame, cooked (GI: 18)
- 1/4 cup almond flakes, toasted (GI: 15)
- 2 green onions, sliced (GI: 15)
- Fresh cilantro, chopped (for garnish)

FOR THE GINGER PEANUT DRESSING:

- 3 tbsp peanut butter (GI: 15)
- 2 tbsp rice vinegar (GI: 15)
- 1 tbsp soy sauce (GI: 20)
- 1 tsp sesame oil (GI: 35)
- 1 garlic clove, minced (GI: 35)
- 1-inch piece of ginger, grated (GI: 0)
- 2-3 tbsp water (to thin, as needed) (GI: 0)

CHAPTER 11. VEGGIE DELIGHTS & SAVORY SIDES

In this chapter, we explore a variety of vegetable-based dishes and savory sides that are perfect for those managing diabetes. These recipes are designed to be both nutritious and delicious, allowing you to enjoy the foods you love while keeping blood sugar levels in check.

Modern nutritional guidelines for diabetes no longer require eliminating foods like pasta, potatoes, and other grains and starchy vegetables. Instead, the focus is on moderation and mindful preparation.

Here are some useful tips:

01 Cooking spaghetti al dente results in a significantly lower glycemic index (GI) compared to overcooking it.

02 Baking starchy vegetables is a healthier option than boiling them, as baking retains more nutrients and results in a lower GI.

03 Cooling cooked vegetables or grains before eating can also make a difference. When these foods are cooled, a significant portion of their starch becomes resistant, which doesn't cause a spike in blood glucose levels. Additionally, resistant starches are excellent for feeding gut microbiota and promoting a healthy microbiome.

04 Soaking grains for at least two hours, or even overnight, before cooking can further reduce their GI, making them a better choice for blood sugar management. Moreover, there are plenty of vegetables and grains with naturally low GIs that make excellent sides for any meal. Think of quinoa, barley, and a variety of fresh, colorful veggies.

Another key point to remember is that adding protein, healthy fats, and fiber to your meals can help lower the overall GI and glycemic load of starchy vegetables or grains. This combination slows down the release of sugar into the bloodstream, helping to prevent glucose spikes and providing a lasting sense of fullness.

In this chapter, you'll find a collection of recipes that embody these principles. From hearty grain dishes to savory vegetable sides, each recipe is designed to be both flavorful and diabetes-friendly. Enjoy exploring these veggie delights and savory sides, and discover how easy and satisfying it can be to include more plant-based goodness in your diet.

ONE-PAN COCONUT CHICKPEA CURRY

This one-pan coconut chickpea curry is a delicious, creamy, and comforting dish inspired by Indian cuisine. It's packed with protein-rich chickpeas and flavorful spices, making it a perfect weeknight dinner that's easy to prepare and full of nutritious benefits.

NUTRITIVE VALUE PER SERVING:

- **Calories:** 320 kcal
- **Carbs:** 27g / **Sugars:** 8g / **Fibers:** 7g
- **Proteins:** 8g
- **Fats:** 15g
- **GI:** Low

HERE IS HOW TO MAKE IT:

01 Heat the coconut oil in a large pan over medium heat. Add the finely chopped onion and sauté until translucent, about 5 minutes.

02 Add the minced garlic and grated ginger, and cook for another 1-2 minutes until fragrant.

03 Stir in the chopped red bell pepper and cook for 3-4 minutes until softened.

04 Add the drained chickpeas, diced tomatoes, coconut milk, curry powder, ground cumin, coriander, turmeric powder, and paprika to the pan. Stir well to combine.

05 Season with salt and pepper to taste. Bring the mixture to a simmer, then reduce the heat to low and let it cook for about 15-20 minutes, stirring occasionally, until the curry has thickened and the flavors have melded together.

06 Garnish with chopped fresh cilantro and serve with lime wedges, if desired.

INGREDIENTS SWAPS AND SUBSTITUTIONS:

- Substitute chickpeas with cubed tofu or cooked lentils for a variation.
- Use spinach or kale instead of bell pepper for added greens.
- Replace coconut milk with almond milk for a lighter version.

PREP: 10 min   **COOK:** 25 min   **SERVINGS:** 4

INGREDIENTS YOU WILL NEED:

- 1 tbsp coconut oil (GI: 0)
- 1 medium onion, finely chopped (GI: 10)
- 3 garlic cloves, minced (GI: 30)
- 1-inch piece of ginger, grated (GI: 0)
- 1 red bell pepper, chopped (GI: 15)
- 1 can (15 oz) chickpeas, drained and rinsed (GI: 28)
- 1 can (14 oz) diced tomatoes (GI: 15)
- 1 can (14 oz) coconut milk (GI: 0)
- 2 tsp curry powder (GI: 0)
- 1 tsp ground cumin (GI: 0)
- 1 tsp ground coriander (GI: 0)
- 1/2 tsp turmeric powder (GI: 0)
- 1/2 tsp paprika (GI: 0)
- Salt and pepper to taste (GI: 0)
- Fresh cilantro, chopped (for garnish) (GI: 15)
- Lime wedges, for serving (optional) (GI: 20)

SERVING SUGGESTIONS:

- Serve over a bed of steamed wild rice or with warm naan bread.
- Pair with sautéed greens or a simple cucumber salad for a complete meal.

PREP: 15 min **COOK:** 45 min **SERVINGS:** 4

RAINBOW LENTIL STEW

Packed with low-GI red lentils and an array of colorful vegetables, this stew is not only delicious but also great for maintaining stable blood sugar levels.

NUTRITIVE VALUE PER SERVING (APPROXIMATE):

- **Calories:** 270 kcal
- **Carbs:** 43g / **Sugars:** 11g / **Fibers:** 13g
- **Proteins:** 14g
- **Fats:** 5g
- **GI:** Low

HERE IS HOW TO MAKE IT:

01 Heat the olive oil in a large pot over medium heat. Add the finely chopped onion and sauté until translucent, about 5 minutes.

02 Add the minced garlic, diced sweet potato, and diced celery. Cook for another 5 minutes until the vegetables begin to soften.

03 Stir in the diced red bell pepper and zucchini, cooking for another 3-4 minutes.

04 Add the rinsed red lentils, diced tomatoes with their juice, and vegetable broth to the pot. Stir to combine.

05 Mix in the ground cumin, dried thyme, and bay leaf. Bring the mixture to a boil, then reduce the heat to low and let it simmer, uncovered, for about 30 minutes, or until the lentils and vegetables are tender.

06 Season with salt and pepper to taste. Remove the bay leaf before serving.

07 Garnish with chopped fresh parsley and grated Parmesan cheese.

INGREDIENTS YOU WILL NEED:

- 1 cup red lentils, rinsed (GI: 21)
- 1 tbsp olive oil (GI: 0)
- 1 medium onion, finely chopped (GI: 10)
- 2 garlic cloves, minced (GI: 30)
- 1 sweet potato, diced (GI: 50)
- 2 celery stalks, diced (GI: 15)
- 1 red bell pepper, diced (GI: 15)
- 1 zucchini, diced (GI: 15)
- 1 can (14.5 oz) diced tomatoes, with juice(GI: 15)
- 4 cups vegetable broth (GI: Low)
- 1 tsp ground cumin (GI: 0)
- 1 tsp dried thyme (GI: 0)
- 1 bay leaf (GI: 0)
- Salt and pepper to taste (GI: 0)
- Fresh parsley, chopped (for garnish) (GI: 15)
- Grated Parmesan cheese (for serving) (GI: 27)

INGREDIENTS SWAPS AND SUBSTITUTIONS:

- Substitute red lentils with green or brown lentils for a different texture.
- Add leafy greens like spinach or kale in the last 5 minutes of cooking for extra nutrients.

PORCINI MUSHROOM BARLEY

Barley is a whole grain rich in fiber, which helps to slow down the absorption of glucose, preventing spikes in blood sugar. The earthy flavors of porcini mushrooms combined with the hearty texture of barley make this a satisfying meal.

NUTRITIVE VALUE PER SERVING (APPROXIMATE):

- **Calories:** 260 kcal
- **Carbs:** 38g / **Sugars:** 2g / **Fibers:** 8g
- **Proteins:** 9g
- **Fats:** 6g
- **GI:** Low

HERE IS HOW TO MAKE IT:

01 Soak the dried porcini mushrooms in warm water for 20 minutes until softened. Drain, chop the mushrooms, and reserve the soaking liquid.

02 In a saucepan, bring the vegetable broth and reserved soaking liquid to a boil. Add the barley, reduce heat, cover, and simmer for 40-45 minutes until tender.

03 Heat the olive oil in a large skillet over medium heat. Sauté the chopped onion until translucent, about 5 minutes.

04 Add the minced garlic and fresh mushrooms, cooking for 5 minutes until tender.

05 Stir in the chopped porcini mushrooms and cooked barley. Cook for an additional 5 minutes until heated through.

06 Remove from heat, stir in the grated Parmesan cheese and fresh thyme. Season with salt and pepper to taste.

PREP: 10 min   **COOK:** 50 min   **SERVINGS:** 4

INGREDIENTS YOU WILL NEED:

- 1 cup pearl barley (GI: 25)
- 1 oz dried porcini mushrooms (GI: 15)
- 2 cups vegetable broth (GI: Low)
- 1 small onion, finely chopped (GI: 10)
- 2 cloves garlic, minced (GI: 30)
- 1 cup fresh mushrooms, sliced (GI: 15)
- 1 tbsp olive oil (GI: 0)
- 1/2 cup grated Parmesan cheese (GI: 27)
- 1 tbsp fresh thyme leaves (GI: Low)
- Salt and pepper to taste (GI: 0)

Pearl barley lowers cholesterol, which is great for your heart, and strengthens bones with its high phosphorus and magnesium content.

PREP: 10 min   **COOK:** 45 min   **SERVINGS:** 4

WILD RICE PILAF WITH CRANBERRIES & ALMONDS

Wild rice is a nutritious whole grain that retains its fiber due to minimal processing, unlike white rice. This fiber content helps to slow the release of glucose into the bloodstream, making it an excellent choice for managing blood sugar levels.

NUTRITIVE VALUE PER SERVING (APPROXIMATE):

- **Calories:** 280 kcal
- **Carbs:** 45g / **Sugars:** 12g / **Fibers:** 6g
- **Proteins:** 7g
- **Fats:** 9g
- **GI:** Low

INGREDIENTS YOU WILL NEED:

- 1 cup wild rice (GI: 45)
- 2 1/2 cups vegetable broth (GI: 0)
- 1 tbsp olive oil (GI: 0)
- 1 medium onion, finely chopped (GI: 10)
- 2 garlic cloves, minced (GI: 30)
- 1/2 cup dried cranberries (GI: 64)
- 1/2 cup sliced almonds, toasted (GI: 15)
- 1/2 tsp dried thyme (GI: 0)
- Salt and pepper to taste (GI: 0)
- Fresh parsley, chopped (for garnish) (GI: 15)

INGREDIENTS SWAPS AND SUBSTITUTIONS:

- Substitute dried cranberries with sun-dried tomatoes for a savory twist.
- Use pecans or walnuts instead of almonds for a nutty variation.
- Add sautéed mushrooms or bell peppers for extra vegetables and flavor.

SERVING SUGGESTIONS:

- Serve as a side dish to grilled vegetables or tofu for a complete vegetarian meal.
- Pair with a green salad for a light and nutritious lunch.

HERE IS HOW TO MAKE IT:

01 Rinse the wild rice under cold water. In a medium saucepan, combine the wild rice and vegetable broth. Bring to a boil, then reduce heat to low, cover, and simmer for 40-45 minutes until tender. Fluff with a fork and set aside.

02 While the rice cooks, heat olive oil in a large skillet over medium heat. Sauté the chopped onion until translucent, about 5 minutes.

03 Add minced garlic and dried thyme, cooking for 1-2 minutes until fragrant.

04 Stir in the cooked wild rice, dried cranberries, and toasted almonds. Mix well and heat through for 2-3 minutes.

05 Season with salt and pepper. Remove from heat and garnish with chopped parsley.

GARLIC BUTTER QUINOA

Garlic Butter Quinoa is a flavorful and nutritious side dish perfect for any meal. It is a high-protein grain with a low glycemic index, making it a great option for those looking to control blood sugar levels.

NUTRITIVE VALUE PER SERVING (APPROXIMATE):

- **Calories:** 190 kcal
- **Carbs:** 28g / **Sugars:** 2g / **Fibers:** 3g
- **Proteins:** 6g
- **Fats:** 7g
- **GI:** Low

HERE IS HOW TO MAKE IT:

01 In a medium saucepan, combine the rinsed quinoa, vegetable broth, garlic powder, butter, and a pinch of salt.

02 Bring the mixture to a boil over medium-high heat.

03 Once boiling, reduce the heat to low, cover, and let it simmer for about 15 minutes, or until the quinoa is tender and the liquid is absorbed.

04 Remove the saucepan from the heat and let it sit, covered, for an additional 5 minutes.

05 Fluff the quinoa with a fork and season with salt and pepper to taste. Garnish with chopped fresh parsley before serving.

PREP: 10 min   **COOK:** 20 min   **SERVINGS:** 4

INGREDIENTS YOU WILL NEED:

- 1 cup quinoa, rinsed (GI: 40)
- 2 cups vegetable broth (GI: Low)
- 2 tablespoons unsalted butter (GI: 14)
- 1 teaspoon garlic powder (GI: Low)
- Fresh parsley, chopped (for garnish)
- Salt and pepper to taste

SERVING SUGGESTIONS:

- Serve as a side dish with grilled chicken or fish.
- Pair with roasted vegetables for a complete vegetarian meal.

Quinoa is a top protein source with all 9 essential amino acids, perfect for vegetarians and vegans.

PREP: 15 min   COOK: 20 min   SERVINGS: 4

HERBS & LEMON BULGUR PILAF

Bulgur is a whole-grain wheat product that retains its fiber, resulting in a lower glycemic index. An added tip: Soaking bulgur overnight releases some starch into the water, reducing its glycemic index even further. This trick works for all grains and also speeds up cooking!

NUTRITIVE VALUE PER SERVING (APPROXIMATE):

- **Calories:** 180 kcal
- **Carbs:** 32g / **Sugars:** 2g / **Fibers:** 5g
- **Proteins:** 5g
- **Fats:** 5g
- **GI:** Low

INGREDIENTS YOU WILL NEED:

- 1 cup bulgur wheat, soaked overnight (GI: 48)
- 2 cups vegetable broth (GI: Low)
- 2 tablespoons olive oil (GI: 0)
- 1 small onion, finely chopped (GI: 10)
- 2 garlic cloves, minced (GI: 30)
- 1 teaspoon fresh ginger, minced (GI: Low)
- Zest and juice of 1 lemon (GI: 20)
- 1/4 cup chopped fresh parsley (GI: 15)
- 1/4 cup chopped fresh dill (GI: 25)
- 1/4 cup chopped fresh mint (GI: 3)
- 1 cup baby spinach leaves (GI: 15)
- Salt and pepper to taste
- 1/2 teaspoon ground cumin (GI: Low)
- 1/4 teaspoon ground coriander (GI: Low)

HERE IS HOW TO MAKE IT:

01 Drain and rinse the soaked bulgur wheat.

02 In a medium saucepan, heat the olive oil over medium heat. Add the chopped onion and sauté until translucent, about 5 minutes.

03 Add the minced garlic and ginger, and cook for another 1-2 minutes until fragrant.

04 Stir in the bulgur wheat, vegetable broth, lemon zest, ground cumin, coriander, and a pinch of salt. Bring to a boil, then reduce the heat to low, cover, and simmer for about 15 minutes, or until the bulgur is tender and the liquid is absorbed.

05 Remove the saucepan from the heat and let it sit, covered, for an additional 5 minutes.

06 Fluff the bulgur with a fork and stir in the lemon juice, chopped parsley, dill, mint, and spinach leaves. Season with salt and pepper to taste.

CAULIFLOWER & MUSHROOMS SKILLET WITH GARLIC BUTTER

This is a delightful and healthy dish that compliments any main course, especially for your vegetarian guests. This is the kind of recipe you'll want to have handy for a busy evening when you need something both nutritious and delicious.

NUTRITIVE VALUE PER SERVING:

- **Calories:** 200 kcal
- **Carbs:** 12g / **Sugars:** 5g / **Fibers:** 5g
- **Proteins:** 6g
- **Fats:** 14g
- **GI:** Low

HERE IS HOW TO MAKE IT:

01 Cut the cauliflower into small florets. Slice the mushrooms and finely chop the onion. Mince the garlic.

02 Melt 3 tablespoons of butter in a large skillet over medium heat. Add the finely chopped onion and cook, stirring frequently, until tender, about 2-3 minutes. Add the sliced mushrooms and cook, stirring often, until beginning to brown, about 5 minutes.

03 Stir in the cauliflower florets; season with salt and pepper to taste. Cook, stirring often, until golden and tender, about 5-6 minutes.

04 Stir in the minced garlic and dried thyme until fragrant, about 1 minute.

05 Stir in the vegetable broth, scraping any browned bits from the bottom of the skillet. Let it simmer for a couple of minutes until the liquid reduces slightly.

06 Remove from heat and stir in the remaining 1 tablespoon butter. Adjust seasoning with salt and pepper, to taste.

07 Sprinkle grated Parmesan cheese over the top and let it melt. Garnish with additional chopped fresh parsley before serving.

PREP: 10 min   **COOK:** 20 min   **SERVINGS:** 4

INGREDIENTS YOU WILL NEED:

- 1 medium head of cauliflower, cut into florets (GI: 15)
- 2 cups mushrooms, sliced (GI: 15)
- 1 medium onion, finely chopped (GI: 15)
- 2 garlic cloves, minced (GI: 30)
- 4 tablespoons butter (GI: 14)
- 1 teaspoon dried thyme (GI: 0)
- Salt and pepper to taste
- 1/4 cup vegetable broth (GI: Low)
- Fresh parsley, chopped (for garnish) (GI: 15)
- 1/4 cup grated Parmesan cheese (optional) (GI: 27)

INGREDIENTS SWAPS AND SUBSTITUTIONS:

- Substitute the cauliflower with broccoli for a different flavor profile.
- Add a splash of balsamic vinegar for an extra tangy flavor.

PREP: 30 min   **COOK:** 60 min   **SERVINGS:** 6

INGREDIENTS YOU WILL NEED:

For the vegetable layers:

- 2 large zucchinis, thinly sliced lengthwise (GI: 15)
- 2 large eggplants, thinly sliced lengthwise (GI: 20)
- 2 tablespoons olive oil (GI: 0)
- Salt and pepper to taste

For the tomato salsa:

- 2 cans (14.5 oz each) diced tomatoes in juice (GI: 35)
- 2 garlic cloves, minced (GI: 30)
- 1 teaspoon dried oregano (GI: 0)
- 1 teaspoon dried basil (GI: 0)
- Salt and pepper to taste (GI: 0)

For the cheese layers:

- 2 cups shredded mozzarella cheese (GI: 20)
- 1/2 cup grated Parmesan cheese (GI: 27)
- Fresh basil leaves for garnish (GI: 0)

INGREDIENTS SWAPS AND SUBSTITUTIONS:

- For a lower-fat version, use cottage cheese mixed with spices and garlic instead of mozzarella.

- Add other vegetables like bell peppers or mushrooms to the layers for added flavor and nutrients.

NO PASTA VEGETABLE LASAGNA WITH MOZZARELLA AND TOMATO SALSA

NUTRITIVE VALUE PER SERVING (APPROXIMATE):

- **Calories:** 300 kcal
- **Carbs:** 15g / **Sugars:** 7g / **Fibers:** 4g
- **Proteins:** 18g
- **Fats:** 20g
- **GI:** Low

HERE IS HOW TO MAKE IT:

01 **Prepare the Vegetables:**

- Preheat your oven to 400°F (200°C).
- Lay the zucchini and eggplant slices on baking sheets, brush with olive oil, and season with salt and pepper.
- Roast for 15 minutes until tender, then set aside.

02 **Make the Tomato Salsa:**

- In a saucepan, combine the diced tomatoes, minced garlic, oregano, and basil.
- Simmer for 15 minutes until the flavors meld. Season with salt and pepper.

03 **Assemble the Lasagna:**

- In a baking dish, spread a thin layer of tomato salsa.
- Add a layer of roasted zucchini slices, followed by a layer of roasted eggplant slices.
- Sprinkle a layer of shredded mozzarella cheese over the vegetables.
- Repeat the layers, finishing with a generous layer of mozzarella and Parmesan cheese on top.

04 **Bake:**

- Reduce oven temperature to 375°F (190°C).
- Bake the lasagna for 30 minutes until the cheese is bubbly and golden.
- Let it cool for a few minutes before serving.

05 **Garnish and Serve:**

- Garnish with fresh basil leaves before serving.

SAUTEED CABBAGE ASIAN STYLE

This Asian-style sautéed cabbage is a quick and delicious veggie dish for any occasion. The cabbage is tender and slightly sweet, while the bell pepper, carrot, and shiitake mushrooms add vibrant color and texture. Fresh ginger and garlic lend pops of flavor, making this a satisfying and healthy option.

NUTRITIVE VALUE PER SERVING (APPROXIMATE):

- **Calories:** 140 kcal
- **Carbs:** 14g / **Sugars:** 6g / **Fibers:** 4g
- **Proteins:** 3g
- **Fats:** 7g
- **GI:** Low

PREP: 15 min   **COOK:** 15 min   **SERVINGS:** 4

HERE IS HOW TO MAKE IT:

01 Thinly slice the cabbage, bell pepper, and julienne the carrot. Slice the mushrooms, mince the garlic, and ginger.

02 Heat olive oil in a large skillet over medium-high heat. Sauté garlic and ginger for 1 minute.

03 Add bell pepper and carrot, cooking for 3-4 minutes. Add mushrooms and cook for another 2-3 minutes.

04 Stir in the cabbage, cooking for about 5 minutes until tender but still crisp.

05 Add soy sauce and rice vinegar, mix well. Drizzle with sesame oil and season with salt and pepper.

06 Sprinkle with sesame seeds and garnish with cilantro.

INGREDIENTS YOU WILL NEED:

- 1 medium head of cabbage, thinly sliced (GI: 10)
- 1 red bell pepper, thinly sliced (GI: 15)
- 1 large carrot, julienned (GI: 35)
- 1 cup shiitake mushrooms, sliced (GI: 15)
- 2 garlic cloves, minced (GI: 30)
- 1 tablespoon fresh ginger, minced (GI: Low)
- 2 tablespoons olive oil (GI: 0)
- 2 tablespoons soy sauce (GI: 20)
- 1 tablespoon rice vinegar (GI: 15)
- 1 teaspoon sesame oil (GI: 35)
- 1 tablespoon sesame seeds (GI: 35)
- Fresh cilantro, chopped (for garnish)
- Salt and pepper to taste

INGREDIENTS SWAPS AND SUBSTITUTIONS:

- Substitute shiitake mushrooms with button or cremini mushrooms.
- Use apple cider vinegar instead of rice vinegar.
- Add sriracha or red pepper flakes for a spicy kick.

SERVING SUGGESTIONS:

- Serve as a side to grilled chicken, tofu, shrimp, or over steamed rice or noodles.

PREP: 10 min   **COOK:** 10 min   **SERVINGS:** 4

ZESTY GARLIC SESAME BEANS

These zesty garlic sesame green beans are bursting with flavor, enhanced by fresh lemon zest and nutty sesame seeds. They're simple to prepare yet full of vibrant taste. Green beans, with a GI of 15, are a nutritious choice, offering both freshness and fiber for a satisfying side dish.

NUTRITIVE VALUE PER SERVING (APPROXIMATE):

- **Calories:** 70 kcal
- **Carbs:** 8g / **Sugars:** 3g / **Fibers:** 3g
- **Proteins:** 2g
- **Fats:** 3g
- **GI:** Low

INGREDIENTS YOU WILL NEED:

- 1 pound green beans, trimmed (GI: 15)
- 2 tablespoons olive oil (GI: 0)
- 3 cloves garlic, minced (GI: 30)
- 1 teaspoon sesame oil (GI: 35)
- Zest and juice of 1 lemon (GI: 20)
- 1 tablespoon sesame seeds, toasted (GI: 35)
- Salt and pepper to taste

HERE IS HOW TO MAKE IT:

01 Boil green beans in salted water for 3-4 minutes until crisp-tender. Drain and plunge into ice water, then drain again.

02 Heat olive & sesame oils in a skillet over medium heat. Add garlic and cook for 1-2 minutes until fragrant.

03 Add blanched green beans to the skillet and stir-fry for 2-3 minutes until heated through and slightly charred.

04 Drizzle with sesame oil, add lemon zest and juice. Toss gently.

05 Sprinkle with toasted sesame seeds, season with salt and pepper.

SERVING SUGGESTIONS:

- Enjoy these Zesty Garlic Sesame Green Beans as a side dish with grilled chicken, fish, or tofu.
- Add red pepper flakes or sriracha for a spicy kick.

BALSAMIC-PARMESAN SAUTÉED SPINACH

This flavorful sautéed spinach combines the tangy taste of balsamic vinegar with the rich, nutty flavor of Parmesan cheese. It's a quick and delicious side dish perfect for any meal and suitable for those managing overweight and diabetes.

NUTRITIVE VALUE PER SERVING (APPROXIMATE):

- **Calories:** 100 kcal
- **Carbs:** 5g / **Sugars:** 2g / **Fibers:** 2g
- **Proteins:** 4g
- **Fats:** 8g
- **GI:** Low

HERE IS HOW TO MAKE IT:

01 **Prepare the ingredients:** wash and remove the stems from the spinach. Mince the garlic cloves.

02 **Sauté the garlic:** heat olive oil in a large skillet over medium heat. Add the minced garlic and sauté for about 1 minute until fragrant, being careful not to let it burn.

03 **Add the spinach:** add the spinach to the skillet in batches, cooking each batch until wilted before adding more. This should take about 3-4 minutes per batch.

04 **Add balsamic vinegar:** Once all the spinach is wilted, add the balsamic vinegar to the skillet. Stir well to combine and cook for an additional 2 minutes.

05 **Finish with parmesan:** Sprinkle the grated Parmesan cheese over the spinach. Toss to combine and cook for another minute until the cheese is melted and well incorporated.

06 **Season and serve:** Season with salt and pepper to taste. If desired, add a pinch of red pepper flakes for a spicy kick. Serve with lemon wedges on the side for an extra burst of freshness.

PREP: 10 min   **COOK:** 10 min   **SERVINGS:** 4

INGREDIENTS YOU WILL NEED:

- 1 pound fresh spinach, washed and stems removed (GI: L15)
- 2 tablespoons olive oil (GI: 0)
- 3 garlic cloves, minced (GI: 30)
- 2 tablespoons balsamic vinegar (GI: 5)
- 1/4 cup grated Parmesan cheese (GI: 27)
- Salt and pepper to taste
- Red pepper flakes (optional, for a spicy kick)
- Lemon wedges (for garnish)

SERVING SUGGESTIONS:

- Serve this Balsamic-Parmesan Sautéed Spinach as a side dish to grilled chicken, fish, or tofu. It also pairs well with pasta or as a topping for a hearty grain bowl.

INGREDIENTS SWAPS AND SUBSTITUTIONS:

- Substitute spinach with kale or Swiss chard for a different green.
- Use apple cider vinegar instead of balsamic vinegar for a milder flavor.
- Add toasted pine nuts or almonds for extra texture and flavor.

PREP: 20 min   COOK: 40 min   SERVINGS: 4

BAKED SWEET POTATO ITALIAN STYLE

This Italian-inspired baked sweet potato dish combines the earthy flavors of chanterelle mushrooms with a rich carbonara sauce made authentically with egg yolks and Parmesan cheese. It's a wholesome and delicious option for those looking to enjoy a gourmet meal while managing type 2 diabetes.

NUTRITIVE VALUE PER SERVING (APPROXIMATE):

- **Calories:** 220 kcal
- **Carbs:** 28g / **Sugars:** 6g / **Fibers:** 4g
- **Proteins:** 8g
- **Fats:** 9g
- **GI:** Moderate

INGREDIENTS YOU WILL NEED:

- 2 large sweet potatoes, scrubbed and cut in half (GI: 50-70)
- 1 cup chanterelle mushrooms, cleaned and sliced (GI: 15)
- 2 tablespoons olive oil (GI: 0)
- 3 large egg yolks (GI: 0)
- 1 cup grated Parmesan (GI: 27)
- 2 garlic cloves, minced (GI: 30)
- Fresh parsley, chopped (GI: 15), for garnish
- Salt and pepper to taste

INGREDIENTS SWAPS AND SUBSTITUTIONS:

- Substitute chanterelle mushrooms with cremini or shiitake mushrooms if unavailable.
- Use Pecorino Romano cheese instead of Parmesan for a sharper flavor.
- Add a pinch of red pepper flakes to the mushroom sauté for a spicy kick.

SERVING SUGGESTIONS:

- Serve these baked sweet potatoes with a side salad or grilled vegetables for a complete meal. They can also be paired with a lean protein such as grilled chicken or fish.

ALTERNATIVE TOPPINGS:

Greek style:

- Top with a generous spoonful of tzatziki sauce.
- Sprinkle crumbled feta cheese over the top.
- Garnish with chopped fresh dill or parsley.

Mexican style:

- Fill with a mixture of seasoned black beans (cumin, chili powder, and lime juice).
- Add a dollop of guacamole.
- Top with sliced jalapeños.
- Optionally, add chopped cilantro and a squeeze of lime juice.

Mediterranean style:

- Fill with hummus.
- Add chopped cucumbers, tomatoes, red onions, and olives.
- Sprinkle with crumbled feta cheese.

Indian style:

- Fill with a mixture of chickpea curry.
- Add sautéed kale.
- Top with a dollop of yogurt.

HERE IS HOW TO MAKE IT:

01 **Preheat and prepare sweet potatoes:** preheat your oven to 400°F (200°C). Wrap each sweet potato half in foil and place on a baking sheet. Bake for 35 minutes. Unwrap the foil and bake for an additional 5 minutes to allow the sweet potatoes to caramelize slightly.

02 **Prepare the carbonara sauce:** in a bowl, whisk together the egg yolks and grated cheese until well combined. Set aside.

03 **Cook the chanterelle mushrooms:** while the sweet potatoes are baking, heat olive oil in a large skillet over medium-high heat. Sauté the minced garlic for about 1 minute, then add the chanterelle mushrooms. Cook for 5-7 minutes until the mushrooms are tender and golden brown. Season with salt and pepper.

04 **Combine and serve:** once the sweet potatoes are done, remove them from the oven and let them cool slightly. Fluff the insides with a fork. Divide the mushrooms evenly among the sweet potatoes.

05 **Add the carbonara sauce:** quickly pour the egg and cheese mixture over the hot sweet potatoes and mushrooms. The heat from the sweet potatoes will cook the egg yolks and create a creamy sauce. Mix gently to coat evenly.

06 **Garnish and serve:** sprinkle with freshly chopped parsley and additional cheese if desired. Season with extra salt and pepper to taste.

CHAPTER 12. MEATY MAINS: BEEF & LAMB DELIGHTS

You've probably heard many times about the importance of protein in a balanced diet. Protein is crucial for building and repairing muscles and bones, producing hormones (including insulin), and keeping our blood sugar levels stable.

Proteins are made up of amino acids, the building blocks our bodies need to function properly. While the body can produce some amino acids, others, known as essential ones, must be obtained through diet. Meat is a source of these essential amino acids, providing what's known as "complete" protein.

Animal protein, like beef and lamb, provides these complete amino acids and essential vitamins such as B12 and iron. However, too much saturated fat, which can be found in meat, can increase blood cholesterol levels. This is particularly concerning for people with diabetes, as they are at a higher risk for cardiovascular diseases. Therefore, choosing lean cuts like sirloin, tenderloin, or leg of lamb is important while limiting fatty meats like pork.

When preparing meat, healthier cooking methods like grilling, broiling, baking, or steaming are recommended to avoid adding extra fats and to retain nutrients. Additionally, portion control is important. Aim for a serving size of 3 to 4 ounces of meat per meal, roughly the size of a deck of cards.

In this chapter, you'll find various recipes showcasing delicious and nutritious beef and lamb dishes. From tender roasts to flavorful stews, each recipe is designed to be diabetes-friendly and full of flavor. Enjoy exploring these meaty delights and discover how satisfying healthy eating can be!

STUFFED BELL PEPPERS WITH GROUND BEEF, QUINOA, AND TOMATO SAUCE

NUTRITIVE VALUE PER SERVING (APPROXIMATE):

- **Calories:** 250 kcal
- **Carbs:** 22g / **Sugars:** 6g / **Fibers:** 5g
- **Proteins:** 16g
- **Fats:** 12g
- **GI:** Low

HERE IS HOW TO MAKE IT:

01 Preheat your oven to 375°F (190°C).

02 Place the halved bell peppers in a baking dish, cut side up. Bake in the preheated oven for 15 minutes to soften.

03 Cook the quinoa according to package instructions and set aside.

04 Heat olive oil in a large skillet over medium-high heat. Sauté the onion and garlic for 2-3 minutes until fragrant.

05 Add the ground beef to the skillet and cook until browned, about 5-7 minutes. Drain any excess fat.

06 Stir in the cooked quinoa, canned diced tomatoes, oregano, basil, salt, and black pepper. Cook for another 3-4 minutes to combine the flavors.

07 Remove the bell peppers from the oven and carefully stuff each half with the beef and quinoa mixture.

08 Spoon tomato sauce over the stuffed peppers.

09 Return the stuffed peppers to the oven and bake for an additional 10-15 minutes. If using mozzarella cheese, sprinkle it on top of each pepper for the last 5 minutes of baking until the cheese is bubbly and golden.

10 Let the peppers cool for a few minutes before serving.

PREP: 20 min **COOK:** 25 min **SERVINGS:** 4

INGREDIENTS YOU WILL NEED:

- 4 large bell peppers (any color), halved and seeds removed (GI: 15)
- 1/2 pound ground beef (GI: 0)
- 1/2 cup quinoa, rinsed (GI: 53)
- 1 medium onion, chopped (GI: 10)
- 2 garlic cloves, minced (GI: 30)
- 1 cup canned diced tomatoes (GI: 15)
- 1 cup tomato sauce (GI: 15)
- 1 tablespoon olive oil (GI: 0)
- 1 teaspoon dried oregano (GI: 0)
- 1 teaspoon dried basil (GI: 0)
- 1/2 teaspoon salt (GI: 0)
- 1/4 teaspoon black pepper (GI: 0)
- 1/2 cup shredded mozzarella cheese (GI: 32, optional)

SERVING SUGGESTIONS:

- Serve these Stuffed Peppers with green salad or steamed vegetables for a balanced meal.

INGREDIENTS SWAPS AND SUBSTITUTIONS:

- Substitute ground beef with ground turkey or chicken for a leaner option.
- Use brown rice instead of quinoa if preferred.
- Add red pepper flakes for a spicy kick.

PREP: 30 min   COOK: 60 min   SERVINGS: 6

INGREDIENTS YOU WILL NEED:

- 2 large eggplants, sliced into rounds (GI: 15)
- 1 pound ground beef (GI: 0)
- 1 medium onion, chopped (GI: 10)
- 2 garlic cloves, minced (GI: 30)
- 1 cup canned diced tomatoes (GI: 15)
- 1/2 cup tomato paste (GI: 45)
- 1/2 teaspoon ground cinnamon (GI: 0)
- 1 teaspoon dried oregano (GI: 0)
- 1 teaspoon dried basil (GI: 0)
- 1/2 teaspoon salt (GI: 0)
- 1/4 teaspoon black pepper (GI: 0)
- 1/4 cup olive oil (GI: 0)
- 1/4 cup grated Parmesan cheese (GI: 27)

FOR THE BÉCHAMEL SAUCE:

- 4 tablespoons butter (GI: 14)
- 1/4 cup all-purpose flour (GI: 70)
- 2 cups milk (GI: 30)
- 1/4 teaspoon ground nutmeg (GI: 0)
- 1/2 cup grated Parmesan cheese (GI: 27)
- 2 egg yolks (GI: 0)
- Salt and pepper to taste

GREEK MOUSSAKA WITH EGGPLANT, GROUND BEEF, AND BÉCHAMEL

NUTRITIVE VALUE PER SERVING (APPROXIMATE):

- **Calories:** 450 kcal
- **Carbs:** 22g / **Sugars:** 8g / **Fibers:** 6g
- **Proteins:** 25g
- **Fats:** 30g
- **GI:** Low

HERE IS HOW TO MAKE IT:

01 Preheat your oven to 375°F (190°C). Arrange the eggplant slices on a baking sheet, brush both sides with olive oil, and bake for 15-20 minutes until softened and lightly browned.

02 While the eggplant is baking, heat 2 tablespoons of olive oil in a large skillet over medium-high heat. Sauté the onion and garlic for 2-3 minutes until fragrant.

03 Add the ground beef to the skillet and cook until browned, about 7-8 minutes. Drain any excess fat.

04 Stir in the canned diced tomatoes, tomato paste, cinnamon, oregano, basil, salt, and black pepper. Simmer for 10 minutes until the sauce thickens.

05 To make the béchamel sauce, melt butter in a saucepan over medium heat. Whisk in flour and cook until golden, about 1-2 minutes. Gradually add milk, whisking to avoid lumps. Cook until thickened, about 5-7 minutes. Remove from heat, stir in nutmeg and Parmesan, let cool slightly, then whisk in egg yolks. Season with salt and pepper.

06 In a greased baking dish, layer half the eggplant slices, spread meat sauce evenly, then add another layer of eggplant slices on top.

07 Pour the béchamel sauce over the eggplant and spread evenly. Sprinkle with Parmesan cheese.

08 Bake in the preheated oven for 30-35 minutes until golden and bubbly. Let cool before serving.

ITALIAN MEATBALLS WITH MARINARA SAUCE AND PARMESAN

PREP: 20 min   **COOK:** 40 min   **SERVINGS:** 4

NUTRITIVE VALUE PER SERVING (APPROXIMATE):

- **Calories:** 350 kcal
- **Carbs:** 10g / **Sugars:** 6g / **Fibers:** 4g
- **Proteins:** 28g
- **Fats:** 28g
- **GI:** Low

HERE IS HOW TO MAKE IT:

01 Combine ground beef, ground pork, almond flour, Parmesan, garlic, parsley, egg, salt, and pepper. Form into meatballs.

02 Brown meatballs in olive oil until all sides are browned, then set aside.

03 For the sauce, sauté onion and garlic in olive oil until fragrant. Add crushed tomatoes, oregano, basil, salt, pepper, and optional red pepper flakes. Simmer for 10 minutes.

04 Add browned meatballs to the sauce and simmer for 20 minutes. Stir in fresh basil before serving.

SERVING SUGGESTIONS:

- Serve these Italian Meatballs With Marinara Sauce over zucchini noodles or cauliflower mash. Sprinkle with grated Parmesan cheese and garnish with fresh basil leaves.

INGREDIENTS SWAPS AND SUBSTITUTIONS:

- Substitute ground pork with ground turkey for a leaner option.
- Use ground flaxseed instead of almond flour for another low-GI alternative.
- Add a pinch of red pepper flakes to the meatball mixture for a spicy kick.

INGREDIENTS YOU WILL NEED:

- 1 pound ground beef (GI: 0) seeds removed (GI: 15)
- 1/2 pound ground pork (GI: 0)
- 1/2 cup almond flour (GI: 25)
- 1/4 cup grated Parmesan cheese (GI: 27)
- 2 garlic cloves, minced (GI: 30)
- 1/4 cup chopped fresh parsley (GI: 15)
- 1 egg, beaten (GI: 0)
- 1/2 teaspoon salt (GI: 0)
- 1/4 teaspoon black pepper (GI: 0)
- 2 tablespoons olive oil (GI: 0)

For Serving:

- 1/4 cup grated Parmesan cheese (GI: 27)
- Fresh basil leaves for garnish (GI: 0)

FOR THE MARINARA SAUCE:

- 2 tablespoons olive oil (GI: 0)
- 1 medium onion, chopped (GI: 10)
- 3 garlic cloves, minced (GI: 30)
- 1 can (28 ounces) crushed tomatoes (GI: 15)
- 1 teaspoon dried oregano (GI: 0)
- 1 teaspoon dried basil (GI: 0)
- 1/2 teaspoon salt (GI: 0)
- 1/4 teaspoon black pepper (GI: 0)
- 1/4 teaspoon red pepper flakes (optional) (GI: 0)
- 1/4 cup chopped fresh basil (GI: 0)

PREP: 30 min **COOK:** 60 min **SERVINGS:** 6

CLASSIC MEATLOAF WITH GROUND BEEF, ONIONS, AND EGG

This classic meatloaf, featuring ground beef, onions, and a surprise egg center, is a protein-rich dish perfect for meal prep. Ideal for those looking to prepare hearty, nutritious meals in advance, it can be easily sliced and served throughout the week.

NUTRITIVE VALUE PER SERVING (APPROXIMATE):

- **Calories:** 350 kcal
- **Carbs:** 8g / **Sugars:** 4g / **Fibers:** 2g
- **Proteins:** 28g
- **Fats:** 24g
- **GI:** Low

INGREDIENTS YOU WILL NEED:

- 1 1/2 pounds ground beef (GI: 0)
- 1 medium onion, finely chopped (GI: 10)
- 2 garlic cloves, minced (GI: 30)
- 1/2 cup almond flour (GI: 25)
- 1/4 cup grated Parmesan cheese (GI: 27)
- 1/4 cup chopped fresh parsley (GI: 15)
- 1 egg, beaten (GI: 0)
- 3 hard-boiled eggs, peeled (GI: 0)
- 1/2 teaspoon salt (GI: 0)
- 1/4 teaspoon black pepper (GI: 0)
- 2 tablespoons olive oil (GI: 0)
- 1/4 cup ketchup (GI: 50)
- 1 tablespoon Worcestershire sauce (GI: 50)

INGREDIENTS SWAPS AND SUBSTITUTIONS:

- Substitute ground beef with ground turkey or chicken for a leaner option.
- Use ground flaxseed instead of almond flour for another low-GI alternative.
- Add finely chopped bell peppers or carrots to the meat mixture for extra vegetables.

SERVING SUGGESTIONS:

- Serve slices of this meatloaf with a side of steamed vegetables or a fresh salad.

HERE IS HOW TO MAKE IT:

01 Preheat your oven to 350°F (175°C). In a large bowl, combine the ground beef, chopped onion, minced garlic, almond flour, Parmesan, parsley, beaten egg, salt, and pepper.

02 Mix until well combined. Place half of the meat mixture in a greased loaf pan and press down to form the bottom layer.

03 Arrange the hard-boiled eggs in a line down the center of the meat mixture.

04 Cover the eggs with the remaining meat mixture, pressing down and shaping it into a loaf.

05 In a small bowl, mix the ketchup and Worcestershire sauce. Spread this mixture evenly over the top of the meatloaf.

06 Bake in the preheated oven for 60 minutes, or until the meatloaf is cooked through and the top is nicely glazed.

07 Let the meatloaf rest for 10 minutes before slicing and serving.

TIPS:

It's also great for meal prep; slice it into portions and store in the refrigerator for up to 5 days.

INDIAN LAMB CURRY WITH SPINACH AND SPICES

Indian lamb curry with spinach and spices is a flavorful and hearty dish, rich in spices and nutrients. This protein-packed curry is perfect for a cozy dinner and pairs well with a variety of low-GI sides.

NUTRITIVE VALUE PER SERVING (APPROXIMATE):

- **Calories:** 400 kcal
- **Carbs:** 14g / **Sugars:** 6g / **Fibers:** 3g
- **Proteins:** 32g
- **Fats:** 25g
- **GI:** Low

PREP: 20 min   **COOK:** 60 min   **SERVINGS:** 4

HERE IS HOW TO MAKE IT:

01 Heat olive oil in a large pot over medium heat. Sauté onion until translucent, about 5 minutes. Add garlic and ginger, cook for 2 minutes.

02 Add lamb cubes and brown on all sides, about 5-7 minutes.

03 Stir in cumin, coriander, turmeric, garam masala, chili powder, salt, and black pepper. Cook for 2 minutes.

04 Add diced tomatoes and water. Bring to a simmer, cover, and cook for 40 minutes, stirring occasionally.

05 Stir in chopped spinach and cook until wilted, about 5 minutes. Remove from heat.

06 Stir in Greek yogurt until well combined. Serve hot.

INGREDIENTS YOU WILL NEED:

- 1 1/2 pounds lamb shoulder, cut into cubes (GI: 0)
- 2 tablespoons olive oil (GI: 0)
- 1 large onion, finely chopped (GI: 10)
- 3 garlic cloves, minced (GI: 30)
- 1 tablespoon fresh ginger, minced (GI: 0)
- 1 can (14.5 ounces) diced tomatoes (GI: 15)
- 4 cups fresh spinach, chopped (GI: 15)
- 1 cup plain Greek yogurt (GI: 35)
- 1 teaspoon ground cumin (GI: 0)
- 1 teaspoon ground coriander (GI: 0)
- 1 teaspoon ground turmeric (GI: 0)
- 1 teaspoon garam masala (GI: 0)
- 1/2 teaspoon chili powder (GI: 0)
- 1/2 teaspoon salt (GI: 0)
- 1/4 teaspoon black pepper (GI: 0)
- 1/2 cup water (GI: 0)

INGREDIENTS SWAPS AND SUBSTITUTIONS:

- Substitute lamb with chicken or beef for a different protein.
- Use kale instead of spinach if preferred.
- Add more chili powder for extra heat.

Lamb is easier to digest than beef and pork, making it a good option for those with digestive issues

PREP: 15 min   COOK: 15 min   SERVINGS: 4

GINGER BEEF STIR-FRY WITH PEPPERS

This ginger beef stir-fry with peppers is an excellent choice for quick, nutritious meals that don't compromise flavor. Its bright colors and rich flavors make it a family favorite.

NUTRITIVE VALUE PER SERVING (APPROXIMATE):

- **Calories:** 320 kcal
- **Carbs:** 12g / **Sugars:** 6g / **Fibers:** 3g
- **Proteins:** 28g
- **Fats:** 16g
- **GI:** Low

HERE IS HOW TO MAKE IT:

01 In a bowl, combine sliced beef with soy sauce and cornstarch. Mix well and let it marinate for 10 minutes.

02 Heat vegetable oil in a large skillet or wok over medium-high heat. Add beef and stir-fry until browned, about 3-4 minutes. Remove beef and set aside.

03 In the same skillet, add bell peppers and onion. Stir-fry for 3-4 minutes until tender-crisp.

04 Add garlic and ginger, stir-fry for 1-2 minutes until fragrant.

05 Return beef to the skillet. Add beef broth, oyster sauce, rice vinegar, and sesame oil. Stir well and cook for another 2-3 minutes until the sauce thickens.

06 Garnish with sliced green onions and sesame seeds before serving.

INGREDIENTS YOU WILL NEED:

- 1 pound beef sirloin, thinly sliced (GI: 0)
- 2 tablespoons soy sauce (GI: 20)
- 1 tablespoon cornstarch (GI: 85)
- 2 tablespoons vegetable oil (GI: 0)
- 1 red bell pepper, thinly sliced (GI: 15)
- 1 green bell pepper, thinly sliced (GI: 15)
- 1 yellow bell pepper, thinly sliced (GI: 15)
- 1 medium onion, thinly sliced (GI: 10)
- 3 garlic cloves, minced (GI: 30)
- 2 tablespoons fresh ginger, minced (GI: 0)
- 1/4 cup beef broth (GI: 0)
- 2 tablespoons oyster sauce (GI: 20)
- 1 tablespoon rice vinegar (GI: 15)
- 1 teaspoon sesame oil (GI: 35)
- 2 green onions, sliced (GI: 10)
- Sesame seeds for garnish (GI: 35)

SERVING SUGGESTIONS:

- Serve this Ginger Beef Stir-Fry With Peppers over cauliflower rice or alongside steamed broccoli for a low-GI meal.

INGREDIENTS SWAPS AND SUBSTITUTIONS:

- Substitute beef with chicken or tofu for a different protein.
- Use tamari or coconut aminos instead of soy sauce for a gluten-free option.
- Add a pinch of red pepper flakes for extra heat.

HERB-CRUSTED RABBIT LEGS IN CREAMY GARLIC SAUCE

NUTRITIVE VALUE PER SERVING (APPROXIMATE):

- **Calories:** 450 kcal
- **Carbs:** 10g / **Sugars:** 3g / **Fibers:** 1g
- **Proteins:** 30g
- **Fats:** 28g
- **GI:** Low

HERE IS HOW TO MAKE IT:

01 Preheat your oven to 375°F (190°C). Heat olive oil in a large oven-safe skillet over medium-high heat. Brown the rabbit legs on all sides, about 5-7 minutes. Remove and set aside.

02 In the same skillet, add the whole garlic heads, cut side down, and cook for 2-3 minutes until golden.

03 Add the chopped onion and sauté until translucent, about 5 minutes. Pour in the white wine, scraping up any browned bits from the bottom of the skillet. Bring to a simmer and cook until the wine is reduced by half, about 5 minutes.

04 Stir in the chicken broth, heavy cream, Dijon mustard, thyme, rosemary, tarragon, salt, and pepper. Mix well to combine.

05 Return the rabbit legs to the skillet, nestling them among the garlic heads. Spoon some of the sauce over the rabbit.

06 Transfer the skillet to the preheated oven and bake for 40-45 minutes, until the rabbit legs are tender and the sauce is bubbly.

07 Garnish with chopped fresh parsley before serving.

SERVING SUGGESTIONS:

- Serve these Herb-Crusted Rabbit Legs With Creamy Garlic Sauce alongside mashed cauliflower or roasted vegetables for a delicious low-GI meal.

PREP: 20 min **COOK:** 60 min **SERVINGS:** 4

INGREDIENTS YOU WILL NEED:

- 4 rabbit legs (GI: 0)
- 2 tablespoons olive oil (GI: 0)
- 2 whole garlic heads, tops trimmed (GI: 30)
- 1 medium onion, finely chopped (GI: 10)
- 1 cup dry white wine (GI: 30-40)
- 1 cup chicken broth (GI: 40)
- 1 cup heavy cream (GI: 30)
- 2 tablespoons Dijon mustard (GI: 35)
- 2 teaspoons fresh thyme leaves (GI: 0)
- 2 teaspoons fresh rosemary leaves (GI: 0)
- 1 teaspoon fresh tarragon leaves (GI: 0)
- 1/2 teaspoon salt (GI: 0)
- 1/4 teaspoon black pepper (GI: 0)
- 2 tablespoons chopped fresh parsley (GI: 15)

INGREDIENTS SWAPS AND SUBSTITUTIONS:

- Substitute rabbit legs with chicken thighs if preferred.
- Use a mix of fresh and dried herbs for convenience.
- Add a splash of lemon juice for a bright, tangy flavor.

PREP: 15 min   **COOK:** 60 min   **SERVINGS:** 6

PEPPER & GARLIC CRUSTED SIRLOIN ROAST

Pepper & garlic crusted sirloin roast is a savory and elegant dish, perfect for special dinners or family gatherings. The robust flavors of freshly cracked pepper and garlic combine to create a delectable crust on a tender sirloin roast.

NUTRITIVE VALUE PER SERVING (APPROXIMATE):

- **Calories:** 350 kcal
- **Carbs:** 2g / **Sugars:** 0g / **Fibers:** 0g
- **Proteins:** 38g
- **Fats:** 20g
- **GI:** Low

INGREDIENTS YOU WILL NEED:

- 3-pound sirloin roast (GI: 0)
- 2 tablespoons olive oil (GI: 0)
- 6 garlic cloves, minced (GI: 30)
- 2 tablespoons freshly cracked black pepper (GI: 0)
- 1 tablespoon sea salt (GI: 0)
- 1 tablespoon fresh rosemary, chopped (GI: 0)
- 1 tablespoon fresh thyme, chopped (GI: 0)
- 1 teaspoon Dijon mustard (GI: 35)

INGREDIENTS SWAPS AND SUBSTITUTIONS:

- Substitute sirloin roast with ribeye roast for a richer flavor.
- Use dried herbs if fresh herbs are not available.
- Add a touch of red pepper flakes to the garlic and herb paste for a hint of heat.

HERE IS HOW TO MAKE IT:

01 Preheat your oven to 375°F (190°C). In a small bowl, combine minced garlic, cracked black pepper, sea salt, rosemary, thyme, and olive oil to form a paste.

02 Rub the Dijon mustard evenly over the sirloin roast. Then, coat the roast with the garlic and herb paste, pressing it firmly to adhere.

03 Place the roast on a rack in a roasting pan. Roast in the preheated oven for about 1 hour, or until the internal temperature reaches 135°F (57°C) for medium-rare.

04 Remove the roast from the oven and cover loosely with foil. Let it rest for 15 minutes before slicing to allow the juices to redistribute.

GOURMET BEEF BURGER WITH PORTOBELLO MUSHROOMS, CARAMELIZED ONIONS, BLUE CHEESE, AND ARUGULA

NUTRITIVE VALUE PER SERVING (APPROXIMATE):

- **Calories:** 480 kcal
- **Carbs:** 14g / **Sugars:** 6g / **Fibers:** 4g
- **Proteins:** 30g
- **Fats:** 34g
- **GI:** Low

HERE IS HOW TO MAKE IT:

01 Preheat the grill to medium-high heat. Brush the Portobello mushroom caps with olive oil and season with salt and pepper.

02 In a bowl, mix the ground beef with Worcestershire sauce, garlic powder, onion powder, salt, and black pepper. Form into 4 patties.

03 Grill the mushroom caps for about 5-7 minutes on each side until tender. Grill the beef patties for 4-5 minutes on each side, or until they reach desired doneness.

04 Meanwhile, heat the butter in a skillet over medium heat. Add the sliced onions and cook, stirring occasionally, until they are soft and caramelized, about 15-20 minutes. Add balsamic vinegar during the last 5 minutes of cooking.

05 Assemble the burgers: Place a grilled Portobello mushroom cap on a plate, top with a beef patty, a generous amount of caramelized onions, crumbled blue cheese, and fresh arugula leaves. Top with another grilled Portobello mushroom cap.

06 Serve immediately.

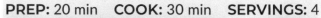

PREP: 20 min   **COOK:** 30 min   **SERVINGS:** 4

INGREDIENTS YOU WILL NEED:

- 8 large Portobello mushroom caps (GI: 15)
- 1 1/2 pounds ground beef (GI: 0)
- 1 tablespoon Worcestershire sauce (GI: 55)
- 1 teaspoon garlic powder (GI: 0)
- 1 teaspoon onion powder (GI: 0)
- 1/2 teaspoon salt (GI: 0)
- 1/4 teaspoon black pepper (GI: 0)
- 2 large onions, thinly sliced (GI: 10)
- 2 tablespoons butter (GI: 14)
- 4 ounces blue cheese, crumbled (GI: 27)
- 2 cups fresh arugula (GI: 0)
- 2 tablespoons balsamic vinegar (GI: 15)
- 2 tablespoons olive oil (GI: 0)

INGREDIENTS SWAPS AND SUBSTITUTIONS:

- Substitute blue cheese with goat cheese or feta for a different flavor profile.
- Use baby spinach instead of arugula if preferred.
- Add a slice of roasted red pepper or avocado for additional texture and flavor.

SERVING SUGGESTIONS:

- Serve these Gourmet Burgers with a side of roasted sweet potato wedges or a fresh mixed green salad for a complete meal.

PREP: 15 min   COOK: 45 min   SERVINGS: 4

BAKED CHILI BEANS WITH GROUND BEEF

Baked chili beans with ground beef is a perfect dish for cozy dinners, offering a rich blend of flavors and hearty ingredients to satisfy the whole family.

NUTRITIVE VALUE PER SERVING (APPROXIMATE):

- **Calories:** 380 kcal
- **Carbs:** 30g / **Sugars:** 6g / **Fibers:** 10g
- **Proteins:** 28g
- **Fats:** 18g
- **GI:** Low

HERE IS HOW TO MAKE IT:

01 Preheat the oven to 375°F (190°C). Heat olive oil in a large skillet over medium-high heat. Brown ground beef, about 5-7 minutes. Drain excess fat.

02 Add onion and garlic; cook until onion is translucent, about 3-5 minutes.

03 Stir in chili powder, cumin, smoked paprika, cayenne (if using), salt, and black pepper; cook for 2 minutes.

04 Add beans, diced tomatoes, tomato paste, and beef broth. Stir well.

05 Transfer to a baking dish, top with shredded cheddar cheese (if desired), and bake for 30 minutes, or until cheese is bubbly and golden brown.

06 Garnish with chopped fresh cilantro before serving.

INGREDIENTS YOU WILL NEED:

- 1 pound ground beef (GI: 0)
- 1 medium onion, chopped (GI: 10)
- 3 garlic cloves, minced (GI: 30)
- 1 can (15 ounces) kidney beans, drained and rinsed (GI: 28)
- 1 can (15 ounces) black beans, drained and rinsed (GI: 30)
- 1 can (15 ounces) pinto beans, drained and rinsed (GI: 39)
- 1 can (15 ounces) diced tomatoes (GI: 15)
- 1 can (6 ounces) tomato paste (GI: 45)
- 1 cup beef broth (GI: 0)
- 2 tablespoons chili powder (GI: 0)
- 1 teaspoon ground cumin (GI: 0)
- 1 teaspoon smoked paprika (GI: 0)
- 1/2 teaspoon cayenne pepper (optional) (GI: 0)
- 1/2 teaspoon salt (GI: 0)
- 1/4 teaspoon black pepper (GI: 0)
- 1 cup shredded cheddar cheese (optional) (GI: 0)
- 2 tablespoons olive oil (GI: 0)
- Fresh cilantro, chopped (for garnish) (GI: 15)

INGREDIENTS SWAPS AND SUBSTITUTIONS:

- Substitute ground beef with ground turkey or chicken for a leaner option.
- Use different types of beans, such as navy beans or cannellini beans, to suit your preference.
- Add diced bell peppers or jalapeños for extra flavor and heat.

SERVING SUGGESTIONS:

- Serve Baked Chili Beans With Ground Beef with a side of cornbread or a fresh green salad for a complete meal.

CHAPTER 13. POULTRY PERFECTION: RECIPES WITH CHICKEN, TURKEY & DUCK

Welcome to a chapter dedicated to the nutritious and versatile world of poultry! For those managing type 2 diabetes, insulin resistance, or striving to lose weight, incorporating chicken, turkey, and duck into your diet can be incredibly beneficial. Poultry is generally lower in saturated fats compared to red meat, making it a heart-friendly choice. It's also rich in essential nutrients and offers a variety of flavors and textures to keep your meals exciting.

As we age, starting around 50, we naturally begin to lose muscle mass—a condition known as sarcopenia. This loss can be worsened by chronic illness, poor diet, and inactivity. Maintaining muscle mass is crucial for mobility and reducing the risk of falls and injuries. Consuming high-quality protein foods, such as lean meats like poultry, helps meet daily protein needs effectively and supports strength and independence.

Combining a protein-rich diet with physical activity, especially strength training, is essential for preserving muscle mass and enhancing overall quality of life.

PREP: 15 min   COOK: 20 min   SERVINGS: 4

CREAMY CHICKEN PAN WITH QUINOA & SPINACH

Creamy chicken pan with quinoa & spinach is a delightful and comforting dish, perfect for any night of the week. This recipe combines tender chicken, low-GI quinoa, and fresh spinach in a creamy, flavorful sauce.

NUTRITIVE VALUE PER SERVING (APPROXIMATE):

- **Calories:** 380 kcal
- **Carbs:** 25g / **Sugars:** 4g / **Fibers:** 3g
- **Proteins:** 28g
- **Fats:** 25g
- **GI:** Medium

INGREDIENTS YOU WILL NEED:

- 1 pound chicken breasts, cut into bite-sized pieces (GI: 0)
- 2 tablespoons olive oil (GI: 0)
- 1 medium onion, finely chopped (GI: 10)
- 3 garlic cloves, minced (GI: 30)
- 1 cup quinoa (GI: 53)
- 2 cups chicken broth (GI: 0)
- 1 cup heavy cream (GI: 30)
- 4 cups fresh spinach, chopped (GI: 15)
- 1/2 cup grated Parmesan cheese (GI: 27)
- 1 teaspoon dried oregano (GI: 0)
- 1/2 teaspoon salt (GI: 0)
- 1/4 teaspoon black pepper (GI: 0)
- Fresh parsley, chopped (for garnish) (GI: 0)

INGREDIENTS SWAPS AND SUBSTITUTIONS:

- Substitute heavy cream with coconut milk for a dairy-free option.
- Use brown rice or barley as alternative grains.
- Add mushrooms or bell peppers for additional vegetables and flavor.

HERE IS HOW TO MAKE IT:

01 Season chicken with salt and pepper. In a large skillet, heat olive oil over medium-high heat. Add chicken pieces and cook until golden brown and cooked through, about 5-7 minutes. Remove and set aside.

02 In the same skillet, add onion and cook until translucent, about 3-4 minutes. Add garlic and cook for 1 minute.

03 Add quinoa, stir to coat, and pour in chicken broth. Simmer until quinoa is tender, about 12-15 minutes.

04 Reduce heat to low. Stir in heavy cream, spinach, Parmesan cheese, oregano, salt, and pepper. Cook until spinach is wilted and sauce thickens, about 2-3 minutes.

05 Return chicken to the skillet, stir to combine, and cook for another 2 minutes to heat through.

06 Transfer to a serving dish and garnish with fresh parsley.

ORANGE AND HERB ROASTED CHICKEN THIGHS

Orange and herb roasted chicken thighs are a delicious and aromatic dish that combines the tangy flavor of orange with the savory notes of herbs and garlic. This recipe is perfect for a comforting and flavorful dinner.

NUTRITIVE VALUE PER SERVING (APPROXIMATE):

- **Calories:** 320 kcal
- **Carbs:** 10g / **Sugars:** 6g / **Fibers:** 2g
- **Proteins:** 25g
- **Fats:** 20g
- **GI:** Low

PREP: 30 min   **COOK:** 45 min   **SERVINGS:** 4

HERE IS HOW TO MAKE IT:

01 In a bowl, mix soy sauce and fresh orange juice. Add chicken thighs, coating them well. Marinate for at least 30 minutes in the refrigerator.

02 Preheat your oven to 400°F (200°C).

03 In a large baking dish, place the marinated chicken thighs, skin side up. Arrange orange wedges, halved garlic heads, and rosemary sprigs around the chicken. Drizzle with olive oil and season with salt and black pepper.

04 Roast in the preheated oven for 45 minutes, or until the chicken is fully cooked and the skin is crispy. Baste the chicken with the pan juices halfway through cooking.

05 Transfer the chicken, oranges, and garlic to a serving platter. Garnish with additional fresh rosemary if desired.

INGREDIENTS YOU WILL NEED:

- 1.5 pounds chicken thighs, bone-in and skin-on (GI: 0)
- 1/4 cup soy sauce (GI: 20)
- 1/2 cup fresh orange juice (GI: 45)
- 2 oranges, sliced into wedges (GI: 45)
- 2 whole garlic heads, halved horizontally (GI: 30)
- 4-5 sprigs fresh rosemary (GI: 0)
- 2 tablespoons olive oil (GI: 0)
- 1 teaspoon salt (GI: 0)
- 1/2 teaspoon black pepper (GI: 0)

PREP: 15 min   **COOK:** 20 min   **SERVINGS:** 4

GARLIC PARMESAN CRUSTED CHICKEN

The savory combination of garlic and Parmesan creates a flavorful crust that pairs wonderfully with tender chicken. This diabetic-friendly version uses almond flour and crushed nuts for a low-GI alternative.

NUTRITIVE VALUE PER SERVING (APPROXIMATE):

- **Calories:** 320 kcal
- **Carbs:** 6g / **Sugars:** 1g / **Fibers:** 2g
- **Proteins:** 28g
- **Fats:** 18g
- **GI:** Low

INGREDIENTS YOU WILL NEED:

- 4 boneless, skinless chicken breasts (GI: 0)
- 1/2 cup grated Parmesan cheese (GI: 27)
- 1/2 cup almond flour (GI: 25)
- 1/4 cup crushed nuts (such as almonds or walnuts) (GI: 15)
- 1 teaspoon garlic powder (GI: 0)
- 1 teaspoon dried oregano (GI: 0)
- 1/2 teaspoon salt (GI: 0)
- 1/4 teaspoon black pepper (GI: 0)
- 2 eggs, beaten (GI: 0)
- 2 tablespoons olive oil (GI: 0)
- Fresh parsley, chopped (for garnish) (GI: 15)

SERVING SUGGESTIONS:

- For a complete meal, serve garlic Parmesan-crusted chicken with a side of roasted vegetables or a fresh green salad.

INGREDIENTS SWAPS AND SUBSTITUTIONS:

- Substitute chicken breasts with chicken thighs for a juicier option.
- Add a pinch of red pepper flakes to the coating mixture for a spicy kick.

HERE IS HOW TO MAKE IT:

01 Preheat your oven to 400°F (200°C).

02 In a shallow dish, combine grated Parmesan cheese, almond flour, crushed nuts, garlic powder, dried oregano, salt, and black pepper.

03 Place almond flour in a separate shallow dish. Coat each chicken breast in almond flour, shaking off any excess. Dip into beaten eggs, then press into the Parmesan almond mixture, ensuring an even coat.

04 Heat olive oil in a large oven-safe skillet over medium-high heat. Add the chicken breasts and cook until golden brown on both sides, about 2-3 minutes per side.

05 Transfer the skillet to the preheated oven and bake for 15-20 minutes, or until the chicken is cooked through and the internal temperature reaches 165°F (74°C).

06 Garnish with chopped fresh parsley before serving.

ROASTED RED PEPPERS, SPINACH & MOZZARELLA STUFFED CHICKEN

Roasted Red Peppers, Spinach & Mozzarella Stuffed Chicken is a delicious and elegant dish perfect for dinner parties or a special family meal. This recipe combines the rich flavors of roasted red peppers, fresh spinach, and melted mozzarella cheese, all stuffed inside tender chicken breasts.

NUTRITIVE VALUE PER SERVING (APPROXIMATE):

- **Calories:** 300 kcal
- **Carbs:** 5g / **Sugars:** 2g / **Fibers:** 2g
- **Proteins:** 35g
- **Fats:** 15g
- **GI:** Low

HERE IS HOW TO MAKE IT:

01 Preheat your oven to 375°F (190°C).

02 Butterfly the chicken breasts by slicing them horizontally but not all the way through, then open them like a book. Season with salt and pepper.

03 Heat 1 tablespoon olive oil in a skillet over medium heat. Sauté garlic for 1 minute, then add spinach and cook until wilted, about 2-3 minutes. Let cool.

04 Layer roasted red peppers, sautéed spinach, and mozzarella cheese on one half of each chicken breast. Fold over and secure with toothpicks.

05 Heat remaining olive oil in the same skillet. Sear the stuffed chicken breasts for 2-3 minutes on each side until golden. Transfer to a baking dish and bake for 20-25 minutes, or until the chicken is cooked through and the internal temperature reaches 165°F (74°C).

06 Remove toothpicks before serving. Serve hot.

PREP: 20 min   **COOK:** 30 min   **SERVINGS:** 4

INGREDIENTS YOU WILL NEED:

- 4 boneless, skinless chicken breasts (GI: 0)
- 1 cup roasted red peppers, sliced (GI: 15)
- 2 cups fresh spinach, chopped (GI: 15)
- 1 cup shredded mozzarella cheese (GI: 22)
- 2 tablespoons olive oil (GI: 0)
- 2 cloves garlic, minced (GI: 30)
- 1 teaspoon dried oregano (GI: 0)
- 1/2 teaspoon salt (GI: 0)
- 1/4 teaspoon black pepper (GI: 0)
- Toothpicks

SERVING SUGGESTIONS:

- Serve Roasted Red Peppers, Spinach & Mozzarella Stuffed Chicken with a side of steamed vegetables or a fresh green salad for a complete meal.

INGREDIENTS SWAPS AND SUBSTITUTIONS:

- Substitute mozzarella cheese with feta or goat cheese for a different flavor.
- Add sun-dried tomatoes for an extra burst of flavor.

PREP: 20 min   **COOK:** 20 min   **SERVINGS:** 4

MEDITERRANEAN SUNDRIED TOMATO CHICKEN MEATBALLS

These meatballs are packed with Mediterranean flavors and can be served with a delicious side of Garlic Butter Quinoa, fresh vegetable salad, or Tzatziki sauce.

NUTRITIVE VALUE PER SERVING (APPROXIMATE):

- **Calories:** 320 kcal
- **Carbs:** 12g / **Sugars:** 4g / **Fibers:** 3g
- **Proteins:** 28g
- **Fats:** 20g
- **GI:** Low

HERE IS HOW TO MAKE IT:

01 In a bowl, mix ground chicken, sundried tomatoes, feta cheese, almond flour, parsley, egg, minced garlic, oregano, salt, and black pepper. Form into 16 meatballs.

02 Heat olive oil in a large skillet over medium heat. Add meatballs and cook, turning occasionally, until browned and cooked through, about 10-12 minutes.

03 Transfer to a serving plate and garnish with additional chopped parsley if desired.

INGREDIENTS YOU WILL NEED:

- 1 pound ground chicken (GI: 0)
- 1/2 cup sundried tomatoes, finely chopped (GI: 35)
- 1/4 cup feta cheese, crumbled (GI: 30)
- 1/4 cup almond flour (GI: 25)
- 1/4 cup fresh parsley, chopped (GI: 15)
- 1 egg, beaten (GI: 0)
- 2 garlic cloves, minced (GI: 30)
- 1 teaspoon dried oregano (GI: 0)
- 1/2 teaspoon salt (GI: 0)
- 1/4 teaspoon black pepper (GI: 0)
- 2 tablespoons olive oil (GI: 0)

SERVING SUGGESTIONS:

- For a complete and delicious meal, serve Mediterranean Sundried Tomato Chicken Meatballs with tzatziki sauce, a fresh vegetable salad, or garlic butter quinoa.

INGREDIENTS SWAPS AND SUBSTITUTIONS:

- Substitute ground chicken with ground turkey or lamb for a different flavor.
- Add chopped olives or capers to the meatball mixture for extra Mediterranean flavor.

PEANUT TURKEY WITH ZUCCHINI NOODLES THAI STYLE

Peanut Turkey With Zucchini Noodles Thai Style is a flavorful and healthy dish that brings the taste of Thai cuisine to your table. This low-carb recipe features tender turkey and zucchini noodles tossed in a savory peanut sauce.

PREP: 15 min   **COOK:** 15 min   **SERVINGS:** 4

NUTRITIVE VALUE PER SERVING (APPROXIMATE):

- **Calories:** 370 kcal
- **Carbs:** 16g / **Sugars:** 3g / **Fibers:** 5g
- **Proteins:** 30g
- **Fats:** 22g
- **GI:** Low

HERE IS HOW TO MAKE IT:

01   Heat olive oil in a large skillet over medium-high heat. Add turkey strips and cook until browned and cooked through, about 5-7 minutes. Remove from skillet.

02   In the same skillet, add minced garlic and cook for 1 minute. Add peanut butter, soy sauce, lime juice, rice vinegar, Stevia syrup, sesame oil, ginger, and red pepper flakes. Stir until smooth and heated through.

03   Add spiralized zucchini noodles to the skillet and toss to coat in the sauce. Cook for 2-3 minutes until noodles are slightly tender. Return turkey to the skillet and mix well.

04   Transfer to serving plates and garnish with chopped peanuts and fresh cilantro.

INGREDIENTS SWAPS AND SUBSTITUTIONS:

- Substitute turkey breast with shrimp or tofu for a different protein.
- Add sliced bell peppers or carrots for extra vegetables.

INGREDIENTS YOU WILL NEED:

- 1 pound turkey breast, sliced into thin strips (GI: 0)
- 4 medium zucchinis, spiralized into noodles (GI: 15)
- 2 tablespoons olive oil (GI: 0)
- 3 garlic cloves, minced (GI: 30)
- 1/2 cup natural peanut butter (GI: 14)
- 1/4 cup soy sauce (GI: 20)
- 2 tablespoons lime juice (GI: 20)
- 2 tablespoons rice vinegar (GI: 15)
- 2-4 drops of Stevia syrup (GI: 0) or 1 tablespoon of honey (GI: 60)
- 1 tablespoon sesame oil (GI: 35)
- 1 teaspoon fresh ginger, grated (GI: 0)
- 1/4 teaspoon red pepper flakes (optional) (GI: 0)
- 1/4 cup chopped peanuts (for garnish) (GI: 7)
- Fresh cilantro, chopped (for garnish) (GI: 15)

SERVING SUGGESTIONS:

- Serve Peanut Turkey With Zucchini Noodles Thai Style with fresh cucumber salad or steamed vegetables.

PREP: 15 min   COOK: 25 min   SERVINGS: 6

TURKEY MEATLOAF MUFFINS WITH BLUE CHEESE

Turkey Meatloaf Muffins with Blue Cheese are a flavorful and convenient twist on classic meatloaf, perfect for meal prep or a quick weeknight dinner. Enjoy these individual-sized meatloaves' convenience and delicious flavor with a creamy blue cheese center.

NUTRITIVE VALUE PER SERVING (APPROXIMATE):

- **Calories:** 200 kcal
- **Carbs:** 5g / **Sugars:** 2g / **Fibers:** 1g
- **Proteins:** 22g
- **Fats:** 10g
- **GI:** Low

INGREDIENTS YOU WILL NEED:

- 1 pound ground turkey (GI: 0)
- 1/2 cup almond flour (GI: 25)
- 1 egg, beaten (GI: 0)
- 1 small onion, finely chopped (GI: 10)
- 2 garlic cloves, minced (GI: 30)
- 1/4 cup tomato paste (GI: 45)
- 2 tablespoons Worcestershire sauce (GI: 50)
- 1 teaspoon Italian seasoning (GI: 0)
- 1/2 teaspoon salt (GI: 0)
- 1/4 teaspoon black pepper (GI: 0)
- 2 ounces blue cheese, cut into small cubes (GI: 27)
- Cooking spray or olive oil (GI: 0)

INGREDIENTS SWAPS AND SUBSTITUTIONS:

- Substitute ground turkey with ground chicken for a different flavor.
- Use crumbled feta or goat cheese instead of blue cheese for a milder taste.
- Add finely chopped bell peppers or carrots for extra vegetables and flavor.

HERE IS HOW TO MAKE IT

01 Preheat your oven to 375°F (190°C). Lightly grease a muffin tin with cooking spray or olive oil.

02 In a large bowl, combine ground turkey, almond flour, beaten egg, chopped onion, minced garlic, tomato paste, Worcestershire sauce, Italian seasoning, salt, and black pepper. Mix until well combined.

03 Divide the mixture evenly into the prepared muffin tin, pressing the mixture down firmly into each cup. Make a small indent in the center of each muffin and insert a cube of blue cheese, then cover it with the meat mixture.

04 Bake in the preheated oven for 20-25 minutes, or until the meatloaf muffins are cooked through and lightly browned on top.

05 Allow the muffins to cool slightly before removing from the tin. Serve warm.

SERVING SUGGESTIONS:

- Serve Turkey Meatloaf Muffins With Blue Cheese with steamed vegetables or a fresh green salad for a complete meal.

TURKEY AND MUSHROOM STROGANOFF

Turkey and Mushroom Stroganoff is a delicious and comforting dish, perfect for a cozy dinner. Enjoy the rich flavors and tender textures in every bite.

PREP: 15 min   **COOK:** 25 min   **SERVINGS:** 4

NUTRITIVE VALUE PER SERVING (APPROXIMATE):

- **Calories:** 350 kcal
- **Carbs:** 12g / **Sugars:** 6g / **Fibers:** 3g
- **Proteins:** 30g
- **Fats:** 20g
- **GI:** Low

HERE IS HOW TO MAKE IT

01 In a large skillet, heat olive oil over medium-high heat. Add ground turkey and cook until browned, about 5-7 minutes. Remove from skillet and set aside.

02 In the same skillet, add chopped onion and cook until translucent, about 3-4 minutes. Add minced garlic and sliced mushrooms and cook until the mushrooms are tender and browned, about 5 minutes.

03 Stir in dried thyme and paprika. Add chicken broth and Worcestershire sauce, stirring to combine. Bring to a simmer and cook for 5 minutes.

04 Reduce heat to low. Stir in Greek yogurt or sour cream until the sauce is smooth and creamy. Season with salt and pepper to taste.

05 Return the cooked turkey to the skillet and mix until everything is well combined and heated through.

06 Garnish with chopped fresh parsley.

INGREDIENTS SWAPS AND SUBSTITUTIONS:

- Use dairy-free yogurt or coconut cream for a dairy-free version.
- Add bell peppers or spinach for extra vegetables and nutrients.

INGREDIENTS YOU WILL NEED:

- 1 pound ground turkey (GI: 0)
- 2 tablespoons olive oil (GI: 0)
- 1 large onion, finely chopped (GI: 10)
- 3 garlic cloves, minced (GI: 30)
- 8 ounces mushrooms, sliced (GI: 15)
- 1 teaspoon dried thyme (GI: 0)
- 1 teaspoon paprika (GI: 0)
- 1/2 cup chicken broth (GI: 0)
- 1 cup Greek yogurt or sour cream (GI: 35)
- 1 tablespoon Worcestershire sauce (GI: 50)
- Salt and pepper to taste (GI: 0)
- Fresh parsley, chopped (for garnish) (GI: 0)
- Mashed cauliflower (GI: 15)

SERVING SUGGESTIONS:

- Serve Turkey And Mushroom Stroganoff over mashed cauliflower for a low-gi option. Pair with a side of steamed vegetables or a fresh green salad.

PREP: 15 min   **COOK:** 20 min   **SERVINGS:** 4

GARLIC AND ROSEMARY DUCK BREAST

Garlic and Rosemary Duck Breast is a simple yet elegant dish, perfect for a special dinner or any occasion. The duck breasts are marinated with garlic and rosemary, then seared to perfection, resulting in a flavorful and succulent meal.

NUTRITIVE VALUE PER SERVING (APPROXIMATE):

- **Calories:** 360 kcal
- **Carbs:** 2g / **Sugars:** 1g / **Fibers:** 0g
- **Proteins:** 28g
- **Fats:** 22g
- **GI:** Low

INGREDIENTS YOU WILL NEED:

- 4 duck breasts, skin on (GI: 0)
- 4 garlic cloves, minced (GI: 30)
- 2 tablespoons fresh rosemary, chopped (GI: 0)
- 2 tablespoons olive oil (GI: 0)
- 1 tablespoon balsamic vinegar (GI: 15)
- 1 teaspoon salt (GI: 0)
- 1/2 teaspoon black pepper (GI: 0)

SERVING SUGGESTIONS:

- Serve Garlic And Rosemary Duck Breast with roasted vegetables or a fresh green salad for a complete meal.

INGREDIENTS SWAPS AND SUBSTITUTIONS:

- Substitute fresh rosemary with thyme for a different herb flavor.
- Use a splash of red wine instead of balsamic vinegar for a richer taste.
- Add a drizzle of Stevia (GI: 0) for a touch of sweetness (optional).

HERE IS HOW TO MAKE IT:

01 In a bowl, combine minced garlic, chopped rosemary, olive oil, balsamic vinegar, salt, and black pepper. Score the skin of the duck breasts in a crisscross pattern and rub the marinade all over the duck breasts. Marinate in the refrigerator for at least 30 minutes, or up to 4 hours.

02 Preheat your oven to 400°F (200°C).

03 Heat a skillet over medium-high heat. Place the duck breasts skin-side down in the skillet and cook for 5-7 minutes, until the skin is crispy and golden brown. Turn the duck breasts over and cook for an additional 2 minutes.

04 Transfer the duck breasts to a baking dish, skin-side up. Bake in the preheated oven for 8-10 minutes, or until the internal temperature reaches 135°F (57°C) for medium-rare.

05 Let the duck breasts rest for 5 minutes before slicing. Serve warm.

ASIAN-INSPIRED DUCK LETTUCE WRAPS

Asian-inspired duck lettuce wraps are a fresh and flavorful dish perfect for a light lunch or dinner. Tender duck is combined with a savory sauce and wrapped in crisp lettuce leaves, making a delicious and healthy meal.

NUTRITIVE VALUE PER SERVING (APPROXIMATE):

- **Calories:** 310 kcal
- **Carbs:** 12g / **Sugars:** 4g / **Fibers:** 3g
- **Proteins:** 25g
- **Fats:** 20g
- **GI:** Low

HERE IS HOW TO MAKE IT:

01 Heat sesame oil in a large skillet over medium-high heat. Add the chopped duck breast and cook until browned and cooked through, about 5-7 minutes.

02 Add minced garlic and grated ginger to the skillet, cooking for 1-2 minutes until fragrant.

03 In a small bowl, mix soy sauce, hoisin sauce, rice vinegar, and stevia. Pour the sauce into the skillet and stir to coat the duck evenly.

04 Stir in the sliced green onions, grated carrot, and chopped cilantro. Cook for an additional 2-3 minutes until heated through.

05 Spoon the duck mixture into the center of each lettuce leaf. Garnish with sesame seeds.

PREP: 20 min   **COOK:** 15 min   **SERVINGS:** 4

INGREDIENTS YOU WILL NEED:

- 1 pound duck breast, skin removed and finely chopped (GI: 0)
- 1 tablespoon sesame oil (GI: 35)
- 3 garlic cloves, minced (GI: 30)
- 1 tablespoon fresh ginger, grated (GI: 0)
- 1/4 cup soy sauce (GI: 20)
- 2 tablespoons hoisin sauce (GI: 35)
- 1 tablespoon rice vinegar (GI: 15)
- 2-4 drops of stevia (GI: 0) or 1 teaspoon of honey (GI: 60)
- 3 green onions, thinly sliced (GI: 10)
- 1 carrot, grated (GI: 35)
- 1/4 cup fresh cilantro, chopped (GI: 15)
- 1 head butter lettuce or iceberg lettuce, leaves separated and washed (GI: 0)
- 1 tablespoon sesame seeds (for garnish) (GI: 35)

INGREDIENTS SWAPS AND SUBSTITUTIONS:

- Substitute duck breast with ground chicken or turkey for a leaner option.
- Use tamari instead of soy sauce for a gluten-free version.
- Add sliced bell peppers or mushrooms for extra vegetables and flavor.

CHAPTER 14. SEA TO PLATE: DELICIOUS FISH & SEAFOOD MEALS

Eating a variety of nutritious foods is essential for everyone, but for people with diabetes, making mindful food choices is crucial. Seafood is a fantastic addition to the diet, offering numerous benefits for heart health and blood sugar management.

People with diabetes are at a higher risk for heart disease, insulin resistance, and inflammation. Omega-3 fatty acids in fish and seafood can help reduce these risks. According to the American Heart Association, omega-3s can lower the risk of heart disease and stroke by 40%.

Fish is not only rich in omega-3 fatty acids but also provides vitamin D, selenium, calcium, phosphorus, and other vital minerals. It's a low-fat, high-quality protein source that supports overall health. Aim to include fish at least twice a week, with each serving about 3.5 ounces of cooked fish. Fatty fish like salmon, mackerel, trout, and sardines are particularly beneficial.

For the best health benefits, grill, broil, or bake your fish to retain its nutritional value without adding extra fats. Including fish in your diet regularly can help manage blood sugar levels and improve heart health, making it an excellent choice for those with diabetes. Dive into these tasty recipes and enjoy the many benefits that fish and seafood bring to your table and your life!

POACHED SALMON IN COCONUT LIME SAUCE

Poached salmon in coconut lime sauce is perfect for a light, refreshing meal that's full of flavor. Enjoy this dish as a healthy weeknight dinner or a special meal to impress your guests.

NUTRITIVE VALUE PER SERVING (APPROXIMATE):

- **Calories:** 350 kcal
- **Carbs:** 8g / **Sugars:** 2g / **Fibers:** 2g
- **Proteins:** 30g
- **Fats:** 20g
- **GI:** Low

PREP: 10 min   **COOK:** 20 min   **SERVINGS:** 4

HERE IS HOW TO MAKE IT:

01 In a large skillet, heat olive oil over medium heat. Add chopped onion and cook until softened, about 3-4 minutes. Add minced garlic and grated ginger, cooking for an additional 1 minute until fragrant.

02 Stir in coconut milk, fresh lime juice, lime zest, fish sauce, soy sauce or tamari, and red pepper flakes (if using). Bring the mixture to a simmer.

03 Season the salmon filets with salt and pepper. Place the salmon filets in the skillet, skin-side down if applicable. Cover and simmer for 10-12 minutes, or until the salmon is cooked through and flakes easily with a fork.

04 Remove the salmon from the skillet and place on serving plates. Spoon the coconut lime sauce over the salmon and garnish with fresh cilantro. Serve with lime wedges on the side.

INGREDIENTS YOU WILL NEED:

- 4 salmon filets (about 6 ounces each) (GI: 0)
- 1 tablespoon olive oil (GI: 0)
- 1 small onion, finely chopped (GI: 10)
- 3 garlic cloves, minced (GI: 30)
- 1 tablespoon fresh ginger, grated (GI: 0)
- 1 can (14 ounces) coconut milk (GI: 45)
- 1/4 cup fresh lime juice (GI: 20)
- 1 teaspoon lime zest (GI: 20)
- 1 tablespoon fish sauce (GI: 0)
- 1 teaspoon soy sauce or tamari (GI: 20)
- 1/2 teaspoon red pepper flakes (optional) (GI: 0)
- 1/4 cup fresh cilantro, chopped (GI: 15)
- Salt and pepper to taste (GI: 0)
- Lime wedges (for serving) (GI: 20)

INGREDIENTS SWAPS AND SUBSTITUTIONS:

- Substitute salmon with cod or halibut for a different fish option.

- Add sliced bell peppers or spinach to the sauce for extra vegetables.

SERVING SUGGESTIONS:

- For a complete meal, serve Poached Salmon In Coconut Lime Sauce with a side of steamed wild rice or cauliflower rice and sautéed greens.

PREP: 20 min   **COOK:** 15 min   **SERVINGS:** 4

GOURMET TUNA PATTIES WITH LEMON CAPER SAUCE

NUTRITIVE VALUE PER SERVING (APPROXIMATE):

- **Calories:** 220 kcal
- **Carbs:** 6g / **Sugars:** 1g / **Fibers:** 2g
- **Proteins:** 22g
- **Fats:** 12g
- **GI:** Low

INGREDIENTS YOU WILL NEED:

For the tuna patties:
- 2 cans (5 ounces each) tuna in water, drained (GI: 0)
- 1/2 cup almond flour (GI: 25)
- 1 egg, beaten (GI: 0)
- 1 small shallot, finely chopped (GI: 10)
- 2 garlic cloves, minced (GI: 30)
- 1/4 cup fresh parsley, chopped (GI: 15)
- 2 tablespoons capers, drained and chopped (GI: 20)
- 1 tablespoon Dijon mustard (GI: 35)
- 1 tablespoon lemon zest (GI: 20)
- 1/2 teaspoon salt (GI: 0)
- 1/4 teaspoon black pepper (GI: 0)
- 2 tablespoons olive oil (GI: 0)

For the lemon caper sauce:
- 1/2 cup Greek yogurt (GI: 35)
- 1 tablespoon capers, drained and chopped (GI: 20)
- 1 tablespoon lemon juice (GI: 20)
- 1 teaspoon Dijon mustard (GI: 35)
- 1 teaspoon fresh dill, chopped (GI: 25)
- Salt and pepper to taste (GI: 0)

HERE IS HOW TO MAKE IT:

01 In a large bowl, combine drained tuna, almond flour, beaten egg, chopped shallot, minced garlic, chopped parsley, chopped capers, Dijon mustard, lemon zest, salt, and black pepper. Mix until well combined.

02 Divide the mixture into 8 equal portions and shape each portion into a patty.

03 Heat olive oil in a large skillet over medium heat. Add the patties and cook for 4-5 minutes on each side, until golden brown and crispy. Remove from skillet and set aside.

04 Make the Lemon Caper Sauce: In a small bowl, whisk together Greek yogurt, chopped capers, lemon juice, Dijon mustard, fresh dill, salt, and pepper.

05 Serve the tuna patties warm, drizzled with lemon caper sauce and a lemon wedge on the side.

INGREDIENTS SWAPS AND SUBSTITUTIONS:

- Substitute almond flour with ground flaxseed for a nut-free option.
- Use lime zest and juice instead of lemon for a different citrus flavor.
- Add a pinch of red pepper flakes to the patties for a touch of heat.

BAKED COD WITH WHITE BEANS

Baked cod with white beans is a simple, hearty, and healthy dish that is perfect for a nutritious meal. Cod is a lean, white fish that is low in fat and high in protein, making it an excellent choice for people with diabetes. Combined with fiber-rich white beans and flavorful tomatoes and herbs, this dish is both satisfying and beneficial for blood sugar control.

NUTRITIVE VALUE PER SERVING (APPROXIMATE):

- **Calories:** 300 kcal
- **Carbs:** 20g / **Sugars:** 5g / **Fibers:** 6g
- **Proteins:** 35g
- **Fats:** 10g
- **GI:** Low

PREP: 15 min   **COOK:** 25 min   **SERVINGS:** 4

HERE IS HOW TO MAKE IT:

01 Preheat your oven to 375°F (190°C).

02 In a large oven-safe skillet, heat olive oil over medium heat. Add chopped onion and cook until softened, about 3-4 minutes. Add minced garlic and cook for another 1 minute until fragrant.

03 Stir in the white beans, diced tomatoes, chicken broth, dried thyme, dried rosemary, salt, and black pepper. Bring the mixture to a simmer and cook for 5 minutes to blend the flavors.

04 Season the cod filets with salt and pepper. Nestle the filets into the bean and tomato mixture in the skillet.

05 Transfer the skillet to the preheated oven and bake for 15-20 minutes, or until the cod is cooked through and flakes easily with a fork.

06 Sprinkle the dish with fresh chopped parsley and serve with lemon wedges on the side.

SERVING SUGGESTIONS:

- Serve Baked Cod With White Beans with a side of steamed vegetables or a fresh green salad for a complete meal.

INGREDIENTS YOU WILL NEED:

- 4 cod filets (about 6 ounces each) (GI: 0)
- 2 tablespoons olive oil (GI: 0)
- 1 medium onion, finely chopped (GI: 10)
- 3 garlic cloves, minced (GI: 30)
- 1 can (15 ounces) white beans, drained and rinsed (GI: 31)
- 1 can (15 ounces) diced tomatoes (GI: 15)
- 1/2 cup chicken broth (GI: 0)
- 1 teaspoon dried thyme (GI: 0)
- 1 teaspoon dried rosemary (GI: 0)
- 1/2 teaspoon salt (GI: 0)
- 1/4 teaspoon black pepper (GI: 0)
- 1/4 cup fresh parsley, chopped (GI: 15)
- Lemon wedges (for serving) (GI: 20)

INGREDIENTS SWAPS AND SUBSTITUTIONS:

- Substitute cod with other white fish like haddock or halibut.
- Use vegetable broth instead of chicken broth for a vegetarian option.
- Add chopped spinach or kale for extra greens and nutrients.

PREP: 15 min   COOK: 15 min   SERVINGS: 4

SHRIMP & ASPARAGUS FOIL PACK

Shrimp & Asparagus Foil Pack is a quick and easy dish perfect for a healthy meal. Shrimp & asparagus foil pack is a quick and easy dish perfect for a healthy dinner. Asparagus is a nutritional powerhouse, rich in fiber, vitamins, and minerals like potassium, which is vital for managing diabetes.

NUTRITIVE VALUE PER SERVING (APPROXIMATE):

- **Calories:** 220 kcal
- **Carbs:** 6g / **Sugars:** 2g / **Fibers:** 2g
- **Proteins:** 24g
- **Fats:** 10g
- **GI:** Low

INGREDIENTS YOU WILL NEED:

- 1 pound large shrimp, peeled and deveined (GI: 0)
- 1 bunch asparagus, trimmed (GI: 15)
- 3 garlic cloves, minced (GI: 30)
- 2 tablespoons olive oil (GI: 0)
- 1 tablespoon lemon juice (GI: 20)
- 1 teaspoon lemon zest (GI: 20)
- 1 teaspoon dried oregano (GI: 0)
- 1/2 teaspoon salt (GI: 0)
- 1/4 teaspoon black pepper (GI: 0)
- 1/4 cup grated Parmesan cheese (optional, for garnish) (GI: 27)
- Fresh parsley, chopped (for garnish) (GI: 15)
- Lemon wedges (for serving) (GI: 20)

INGREDIENTS SWAPS AND SUBSTITUTIONS:

- Substitute shrimp with scallops or chunks of white fish for a different seafood option.
- Use fresh thyme or dill instead of oregano for a different herb flavor.
- Add cherry tomatoes or bell peppers for extra color and nutrients.

HERE IS HOW TO MAKE IT:

01 Preheat your oven to 400°F (200°C).

02 In a large bowl, combine shrimp, minced garlic, olive oil, lemon juice, lemon zest, dried oregano, salt, and black pepper. Toss to coat evenly.

03 Cut four large pieces of aluminum foil. Place the asparagus stalks in the center of each piece of foil. Divide the shrimp mixture evenly among the foil pieces, placing it on top of the asparagus.

04 Fold the sides of the foil over the shrimp and asparagus, sealing the packs tightly to ensure no steam escapes.

05 Place the foil packs on a baking sheet and bake in the preheated oven for 15 minutes, or until the shrimp are cooked through and the asparagus is tender.

06 Carefully open the foil packs (be cautious of hot steam). Transfer the shrimp and asparagus to serving plates. Garnish with grated Parmesan cheese, if desired, and fresh parsley. Serve with lemon wedges on the side.

SERVING SUGGESTIONS:

- For a complete meal, serve the Shrimp And Asparagus Foil Pack with cauliflower rice or a fresh green salad.

MEDITERRANEAN SEAFOOD SAUTÉ

Mediterranean Seafood Sauté is a vibrant and flavorful dish that combines a variety of seafood with fresh vegetables and Mediterranean herbs. It is healthy and easy to prepare, making it perfect for any occasion. Frozen seafood works perfectly, making this a convenient option.

NUTRITIVE VALUE PER SERVING (APPROXIMATE):

- **Calories:** 250 kcal
- **Carbs:** 14g / **Sugars:** 6g / **Fibers:** 4g
- **Proteins:** 28g
- **Fats:** 10g
- **GI:** Low

PREP: 15 min   **COOK:** 20 min   **SERVINGS:** 4

HERE IS HOW TO MAKE IT:

01 Rinse and pat dry the shrimp, scallops, and calamari. Set aside.

02 In a large skillet, heat olive oil over medium-high heat. Add onion and cook until softened, about 3-4 minutes. Add garlic and cook for 1 minute.

03 Add bell peppers and cherry tomatoes. Cook for 5 minutes until tender.

04 Add shrimp, scallops, and calamari to the skillet. Stir in diced tomatoes, tomato paste, white wine (if using), oregano, thyme, red pepper flakes, salt, and pepper. Cover and cook until the shrimp and scallops are opaque, about 5-7 minutes.

05 Transfer to a serving dish. Garnish with parsley and serve with lemon wedges.

INGREDIENTS SWAPS AND SUBSTITUTIONS:

- Substitute white wine with chicken broth for a non-alcoholic option.
- Use other vegetables like spinach or kale for added variety.
- Add a splash of balsamic vinegar for extra flavor.

INGREDIENTS YOU WILL NEED:

- 1/2 pound shrimp, peeled and deveined (GI: 0)
- 1/2 pound scallops (GI: 0)
- 1/2 pound calamari, sliced into rings (GI: 0)
- 2 tablespoons olive oil (GI: 0)
- 1 large onion, chopped (GI: 10)
- 3 garlic cloves, minced (GI: 30)
- 1 red bell pepper, sliced (GI: 15)
- 1 yellow bell pepper, sliced (GI: 15)
- 1/2 cup cherry tomatoes, halved (GI: 15)
- 1 can (15 ounces) diced tomatoes (GI: 15)
- 2 tablespoons tomato paste (GI: 30)
- 1/2 cup white wine (optional) (GI: 30-40)
- 1 teaspoon dried oregano (GI: 0)
- 1 teaspoon dried thyme (GI: 0)
- 1/2 teaspoon red pepper flakes (optional) (GI: 0)
- Salt and pepper to taste (GI: 0)
- 1/4 cup fresh parsley, chopped (GI: 15)
- Lemon wedges (for serving) (GI: 20)

SERVING SUGGESTIONS:

- Serve Mediterranean Seafood Sauté with eggplant chips or toasted thin slices of whole grain bread for a complete meal.

PREP: 15 min   **COOK:** 15 min   **SERVINGS:** 4

PISTACHIO CRUSTED HALIBUT

Pistachio Crusted Halibut is an elegant and flavorful dish that's perfect for a special dinner or any occasion. The crunchy pistachio crust complements the tender and flaky halibut, creating a delightful combination of textures and flavors.

NUTRITIVE VALUE PER SERVING (APPROXIMATE):

- **Calories:** 350 kcal
- **Carbs:** 10g / **Sugars:** 2g / **Fibers:** 3g
- **Proteins:** 30g
- **Fats:** 20g
- **GI:** Low to Medium

INGREDIENTS YOU WILL NEED:

- 4 halibut filets (about 6 ounces each) (GI: 0)
- 1 cup shelled pistachios, finely chopped (GI: 15)
- 1/4 cup almond flour (GI: 25)
- 2 tablespoons grated Parmesan cheese (GI: 27)
- 1 tablespoon fresh parsley, chopped (GI: 15)
- 1 teaspoon lemon zest (GI: 20)
- 1/2 teaspoon garlic powder (GI: 0)
- 1/2 teaspoon salt (GI: 0)
- 1/4 teaspoon black pepper (GI: 0)
- 2 tablespoons olive oil (GI: 0)
- 1 egg, beaten (GI: 0)
- Lemon wedges (for serving) (GI: 20)

INGREDIENTS SWAPS AND SUBSTITUTIONS:

- Substitute halibut with other white fish like cod or haddock.
- Use ground flaxseed instead of almond flour for a different texture.
- Add a pinch of cayenne pepper to the crust for a spicy kick.

HERE IS HOW TO MAKE IT:

01 **Preheat the oven:** preheat your oven to 400°f (200°c). Line a baking sheet with parchment paper.

02 **Prepare the crust:** in a bowl, combine chopped pistachios, almond flour, grated parmesan cheese, chopped parsley, lemon zest, garlic powder, salt, and black pepper. Mix well.

03 **Coat the fish:** pat the halibut fillets dry with paper towels. Brush each fillet with a thin layer of olive oil, then dip into the beaten egg. Press each fillet into the pistachio mixture, ensuring an even coat on all sides.

04 **Bake:** place the coated fillets on the prepared baking sheet. Bake in the preheated oven for 12-15 minutes, or until the fish is cooked through and the crust is golden brown.

05 **Serve:** transfer the fillets to serving plates. Serve with lemon wedges on the side.

SERVING SUGGESTIONS:

- Serve Pistachio Crusted Halibut with a side of roasted vegetables or a fresh green salad for a complete meal.

OVEN-BAKED SALMON GREEK STYLE WITH DILL, CAPERS & FETA

Oven-Baked Salmon Greek Style is a delightful dish featuring a whole salmon filet topped with a mixture of fresh dill, capers, and feta cheese. This flavorful and healthy recipe is easy to prepare and perfect for any occasion.

NUTRITIVE VALUE PER SERVING (APPROXIMATE):

- **Calories:** 350 kcal
- **Carbs:** 4g / **Sugars:** 2g / **Fibers:** 1g
- **Proteins:** 35g
- **Fats:** 22g
- **GI:** Low

PREP: 15 min   COOK: 25 min   SERVINGS: 4

HERE IS HOW TO MAKE IT:

01 Preheat your oven to 375°F (190°C).

02 In a small bowl, mix the chopped dill, capers, and olive oil until well combined.

03 Place the salmon filet skin-side down on a baking sheet lined with parchment paper. Season the filet with salt and pepper.

04 Spread the dill and caper mixture evenly over the salmon filet. Arrange the feta cheese cubes on top of the mix.

05 Cover the salmon loosely with aluminum foil and bake in the preheated oven for 15 minutes. Remove the foil and bake for an additional 5 minutes, or until the feta is lightly browned and the salmon is cooked through.

06 Remove the salmon from the oven and let it rest for a few minutes. Cut into portions and serve with steamed asparagus and lemon wedges on the side.

INGREDIENTS YOU WILL NEED:

- 1 whole salmon filet, skin on (about 2 pounds) (GI: 0)
- 2 tablespoons olive oil (GI: 0)
- 1/4 cup fresh dill, finely chopped (GI: 25)
- 2 tablespoons capers, finely chopped (GI: 20)
- 1/2 cup feta cheese, cubed (GI: 30)
- Salt and pepper to taste (GI: 0)
- Lemon wedges (for serving) (GI: 20)

INGREDIENTS SWAPS AND SUBSTITUTIONS:

- Substitute salmon with other fatty fish like trout or mackerel.
- Add sliced cherry tomatoes on top for extra color and flavor.

PREP: 15 min   COOK: 10 min   SERVINGS: 4

GARLIC BUTTER SHRIMP WITH ZUCCHINI NOODLES & CHERRY TOMATOES

Garlic Butter Shrimp With Zucchini Noodles & Cherry Tomatoes is a light and healthy dish that is quick and easy to prepare. This recipe features succulent shrimp sautéed in garlic butter, served with fresh zucchini noodles and cherry tomatoes, making it a perfect low-carb meal.

NUTRITIVE VALUE PER SERVING (APPROXIMATE):

- **Calories:** 250 kcal
- **Carbs:** 8g / **Sugars:** 4g / **Fibers:** 2g
- **Proteins:** 25g
- **Fats:** 14g
- **GI:** Low

INGREDIENTS YOU WILL NEED:

- 1 pound large shrimp, peeled and deveined (GI: 0)
- 4 medium zucchinis, spiralized into noodles (GI: 15)
- 1 cup cherry tomatoes, halved (GI: 15)
- 4 tablespoons butter (GI: 14)
- 4 garlic cloves, minced (GI: 30)
- 1 tablespoon olive oil (GI: 0)
- 1/4 teaspoon red pepper flakes (optional) (GI: 0)
- Salt and pepper to taste (GI: 0)
- 1/4 cup fresh parsley, chopped (GI: 15)
- 1 lemon, cut into wedges (GI: 20)

INGREDIENTS SWAPS AND SUBSTITUTIONS:

- Substitute shrimp with scallops or chicken for a different protein.
- Add a splash of white wine to the garlic butter sauce for extra depth of flavor.

HERE IS HOW TO MAKE IT:

01 Spiralize the zucchinis into noodles and set aside.

02 In a large skillet, heat olive oil and 2 tablespoons of butter over medium-high heat. Add minced garlic and red pepper flakes (if using), and cook for 1 minute until fragrant. Add the shrimp, season with salt and pepper, and cook for 2-3 minutes on each side until pink and opaque. Remove the shrimp from the skillet and set aside.

03 In the same skillet, add the remaining 2 tablespoons of butter. Once melted, add the cherry tomatoes and cook for 2-3 minutes until they start to soften. Add the zucchini noodles, season with salt and pepper, and cook for another 2-3 minutes until the noodles are slightly tender.

04 Return the cooked shrimp to the skillet and toss everything together to combine and heat through. Garnish with fresh parsley and serve with lemon wedges.

THAI GREEN CARY WITH FISH

Thai Green Curry with Fish is a flavorful and aromatic dish that brings the vibrant tastes of Thailand to your table. This curry features tender fish filets simmered in a rich, creamy green sauce made with coconut milk, fresh herbs, and vegetables.

NUTRITIVE VALUE PER SERVING (APPROXIMATE):

- **Calories:** 300 kcal
- **Carbs:** 12g / **Sugars:** 4g / **Fibers:** 3g
- **Proteins:** 28g
- **Fats:** 18g
- **GI:** Low

PREP: 15 min　　**COOK:** 25 min　　**SERVINGS:** 4

HERE IS HOW TO MAKE IT:

01 Heat olive oil in a large pot over medium heat. Add minced garlic and grated ginger, cooking for 1 minute until fragrant. Stir in green curry paste and cook for another 1-2 minutes.

02 Pour in coconut milk and fish or vegetable broth. Stir in fish and soy sauce, bringing the mixture to a simmer.

03 Add red bell pepper, zucchini, and snap peas. Simmer for 5-7 minutes until the vegetables are tender.

04 Gently add the fish chunks, simmering for another 5-7 minutes until the fish is cooked through and flakes easily. Season with salt and pepper to taste.

05 Stir in fresh basil and cilantro just before serving.

INGREDIENTS SWAPS AND SUBSTITUTIONS:

- Substitute white fish with shrimp or chicken for a different protein.
- Use green beans or broccoli instead of snap peas for added variety.

INGREDIENTS YOU WILL NEED:

- 1 pound white fish filets (such as cod or tilapia), cut into chunks (GI: 0)
- 2 tablespoons green curry paste (GI: 0)
- 1 can (14 ounces) coconut milk (GI: 45)
- 1 cup fish or vegetable broth (GI: 0)
- 1 tablespoon fish sauce (GI: 0)
- 1 tablespoon soy sauce (GI: 20)
- 1 tablespoon olive oil (GI: 0)
- 2 garlic cloves, minced (GI: 30)
- 1 tablespoon fresh ginger, grated (GI: 0)
- 1 red bell pepper, sliced (GI: 15)
- 1 zucchini, sliced (GI: 15)
- 1 cup snap peas (GI: 15)
- 1/2 cup fresh basil leaves, chopped (GI: 0)
- 1/4 cup fresh cilantro, chopped (GI: 15)
- 1 lime, cut into wedges (GI: 20)
- Salt and pepper to taste (GI: 0)
- Cooked brown rice or cauliflower rice, for serving (GI: varies)

SERVING SUGGESTIONS:

- Serve Thai Green Curry with Fish with a side of cooked brown rice or cauliflower rice to keep the meal low-GI and balanced.

CHAPTER 15. SMALL BITES, BIG FLAVOR: APPETIZERS & SNACKS

When it comes to snacks, people with diabetes need to consider their individual needs. Some may feel better with three regular meals a day, while others might benefit from healthy snacks. It's important to consult your doctor to determine what's best for you. If you do opt for snacks, they should be low in sugar and rich in fiber, protein, and healthy fats.

In this chapter, you'll find delicious and diabetes-friendly appetizers and snacks that can help keep your energy levels stable and satisfy your cravings. Enjoy these small bites that pack a big flavor punch!

ZUCCHINI PHILADELPHIA ROLL

Zucchini Philadelphia Roll is a fresh and delicious twist on traditional sushi, using a baked zucchini "pancake" as the base. Filled with creamy philadelphia cheese, smoked salmon, and crisp cucumber, these rolls are perfect for a light and healthy meal.

NUTRITIVE VALUE PER SERVING (APPROXIMATE):

- **Calories:** 300 kcal
- **Carbs:** 10g / **Sugars:** 4g / **Fibers:** 2g
- **Proteins:** 18g
- **Fats:** 22g
- **GI:** Low

HERE IS HOW TO MAKE IT:

01 Preheat your oven to 375°F (190°C) and line a baking sheet with parchment paper. Lightly grease the parchment paper with olive oil.

02 Grate the zucchinis and place them in a clean kitchen towel. Squeeze out as much moisture as possible.

03 In a large bowl, combine the grated zucchini, beaten egg, almond flour, salt, and black pepper. Mix well to combine.

04 Spread the zucchini mixture evenly onto the prepared baking sheet, forming a thin, even layer. Bake in the preheated oven for 15 minutes, or until the zucchini pancake is set and lightly browned.

05 **Assemble the roll:** once the zucchini pancake is done, remove it from the oven and let it cool slightly. Spread a layer of philadelphia cream cheese evenly over the zucchini pancake. Arrange the smoked salmon slices evenly over the cream cheese, followed by the cucumber slices.

06 Carefully roll up the zucchini pancake from one end, using the parchment paper to help guide it. Roll tightly but gently to avoid tearing.

07 **Slice and serve:** using a sharp knife, slice the roll into bite-sized pieces, similar to sushi rolls.

PREP: 20 min   **COOK:** 15 min   **SERVINGS:** 4

INGREDIENTS YOU WILL NEED:

- 2 large zucchinis, grated (GI: 15)
- 1 egg, beaten (GI: 0)
- 1/4 cup almond flour (GI: 25)
- 1/4 teaspoon salt (GI: 0)
- 1/4 teaspoon black pepper (GI: 0)
- 1 cup Philadelphia cream cheese (GI: 35)
- 1/2 pound smoked salmon, thinly sliced (GI: 0)
- 1 cucumber, thinly sliced (GI: 15)
- 1 tablespoon olive oil (GI: 0)

INGREDIENTS SWAPS AND SUBSTITUTIONS:

- Substitute almond flour with whole wheat flour or panko breadcrumbs for a different texture.
- Use fresh dill or chives instead of cucumber for a different flavor profile.
- Add a drizzle of sriracha or spicy mayo for a bit of heat.

SERVING SUGGESTIONS:

- Serve Zucchini Philadelphia Roll with soy sauce, pickled ginger, and wasabi for a complete sushi experience. These rolls also pair well with a side of miso soup or a fresh green salad.

PREP: 10 min   COOK: 0 min   SERVINGS: 4

CAPRESE-STYLE STUFFED AVOCADO

Caprese-Style Stuffed Avocado is a fresh and delicious dish that combines the classic flavors of a caprese salad with creamy avocado. This simple and healthy recipe is perfect for a light lunch or an appetizer, served as avocado "boats" with their skins intact.

NUTRITIVE VALUE PER SERVING (APPROXIMATE):

- **Calories:** 300 kcal
- **Carbs:** 12g / **Sugars:** 4g / **Fibers:** 7g
- **Proteins:** 8g
- **Fats:** 26g
- **GI:** Low

HERE IS HOW TO MAKE IT:

01 Halve and pit the avocados. Using a spoon, slightly scoop out some of the flesh to create a larger cavity, but keep the skins intact to form "boats."

02 In a bowl, combine the halved cherry tomatoes, mini mozzarella balls, and chopped basil. Add the pesto sauce and toss gently to combine. Season with salt and pepper to taste.

03 Spoon the Caprese salad mixture into the avocado halves, filling each cavity generously.

04 Place the stuffed avocados on a serving plate. Garnish with additional basil leaves if desired.

INGREDIENTS YOU WILL NEED:

- 2 ripe avocados, halved and pitted (GI: 10)
- 1 cup cherry tomatoes, halved (GI: 15)
- 1 cup mini mozzarella balls (bocconcini) (GI: 20)
- 1/4 cup fresh basil leaves, chopped (GI: 0)
- 2 tablespoons pesto sauce (GI: 20)
- Salt and pepper to taste (GI: 0)

SERVING SUGGESTIONS:

- Serve Caprese Style Stuffed Avocado as a light lunch, appetizer, or side dish. Pair with a fresh green salad or grilled chicken for a complete meal.

Avocados have more potassium than bananas, crucial for maintaining normal blood pressure. Despite their unsweet nature, avocados are technically a fruit, specifically a berry.

DEVILED EGGS WITH THREE UNIQUE FILLING VARIATIONS

NUTRITIVE VALUE (APPROXIMATE):

- **Calories:** 120-150 kcal (depending on the stuffing)
- **GI:** Low

CURRY AND CHUTNEY DEVILED EGGS

INGREDIENTS YOU WILL NEED:

- 6 large eggs, hard-boiled and peeled (GI: 0)
- 3 tablespoons mayonnaise or Greek yogurt (GI: 35-50)
- 1 teaspoon curry powder (GI: 0)
- 2 tablespoons mango chutney (GI: 55)
- Salt and pepper to taste (GI: 0)
- Fresh cilantro, chopped (for garnish) (GI: 15)

PREPARATION:

01 Cut the eggs in half lengthwise and remove the yolks.

02 In a bowl, mash the yolks and mix with mayonnaise or Greek yogurt, curry powder, and mango chutney. Season with salt and pepper.

03 Spoon or pipe the yolk mixture back into the egg whites.

04 Garnish with chopped fresh cilantro.

BACON AND CHEDDAR DEVILED EGGS

INGREDIENTS YOU WILL NEED:

- 6 large eggs, hard-boiled and peeled (GI: 0)
- 3 tablespoons mayonnaise (GI: 50)
- 1 teaspoon Dijon mustard (GI: 35)
- 1/4 cup shredded cheddar cheese (GI: 0)
- 2 slices cooked bacon, crumbled (GI: 0)
- Salt and pepper to taste (GI: 0)
- Chives, chopped (for garnish) (GI: 0)

PREPARATION:

01 Cut the eggs in half lengthwise and remove the yolks.

02 In a bowl, mash the yolks and mix with mayonnaise, Dijon mustard, shredded cheddar cheese,

PREP: 20 min **COOK:** 15 min **SERVINGS:** 4

02 and crumbled bacon. Season with salt and pepper.

03 Spoon or pipe the yolk mixture back into the egg whites.

04 Garnish with chopped chives.

SUN-DRIED TOMATO AND BASIL DEVILED EGGS

INGREDIENTS YOU WILL NEED:

- 6 large eggs, hard-boiled and peeled (GI: 0)
- 3 tablespoons mayonnaise (GI: 50)
- 2 tablespoons finely chopped sun-dried tomatoes (GI: 35)
- 1 tablespoon fresh basil, finely chopped (GI: 0)
- 1/2 teaspoon garlic powder (GI: 0)
- Salt and pepper to taste (GI: 0)
- Basil leaves (for garnish) (GI: 0)

PREPARATION:

01 Cut the eggs in half lengthwise and remove the yolks.

02 In a bowl, mash the yolks and mix with mayonnaise, finely chopped sun-dried tomatoes, fresh basil, and garlic powder. Season with salt and pepper.

03 Spoon or pipe the yolk mixture back into the egg whites.

04 Garnish with small basil leaves.

PREP: 20 min   **COOK:** 0 min   **SERVINGS:** 4

VEGGIE SPRING ROLLS WITH PEANUT SAUCE

Veggie Spring Rolls with Peanut Sauce are a fresh and healthy appetizer or snack. These rolls are packed with colorful vegetables and served with a delicious, creamy peanut sauce. They are perfect for any occasion and make an excellent meal prep option!

NUTRITIVE VALUE PER SERVING (APPROXIMATE):

- **Calories:** 250 kcal
- **Carbs:** 30g / **Sugars:** 10g / **Fibers:** 6g
- **Proteins:** 7g
- **Fats:** 12g
- **GI:** Medium

INGREDIENTS YOU WILL NEED:

For the spring rolls:
- 8 rice paper wrappers (GI: 70)
- 1 cup shredded carrots (GI: 35)
- 1 cup red bell pepper, thinly sliced (GI: 15)
- 1 cup cucumber, thinly sliced (GI: 15)
- 1 cup purple cabbage, thinly sliced (GI: 15)
- 1 cup fresh spinach leaves (GI: 15)
- 1/4 cup fresh mint leaves (GI: 0)
- 1/4 cup fresh cilantro leaves (GI: 15)

For the peanut sauce:
- 1/4 cup creamy peanut butter (GI: 14)
- 2 tablespoons soy sauce (GI: 20)
- 1 tablespoon rice vinegar (GI: 15)
- 2-4 drops of stevia syrup (GI: 0)
- 1 teaspoon sesame oil (GI: 35)
- 1 garlic clove, minced (GI: 30)
- 1 teaspoon fresh ginger, grated (GI: 0)
- Water, to thin as needed

INGREDIENTS SWAPS AND SUBSTITUTIONS:

- Use any combination of fresh vegetables you prefer, such as avocado, radish, or bean sprouts.
- Add cooked shrimp or tofu for extra protein.

HERE IS HOW TO MAKE IT:

01   Prepare the peanut sauce:

- In a small bowl, whisk together peanut butter, soy sauce, rice vinegar, stevia, sesame oil, minced garlic, and grated ginger.
- Add water, one tablespoon at a time, to reach desired consistency.

02   Prepare the spring rolls:

- Fill a large bowl with warm water. Dip one rice paper wrapper into the water for about 10-15 seconds to soften.
- Lay the softened wrapper on a flat surface and place a small amount of shredded carrots, red bell pepper, cucumber, purple cabbage, spinach, mint leaves, and cilantro leaves in the center.
- Fold the bottom of the wrapper over the filling, then fold in the sides, and roll tightly to close. Repeat with remaining wrappers and filling.

03   Serve:

- Arrange the spring rolls on a serving plate and serve with peanut sauce on the side.

SERVING SUGGESTIONS:

- Veggie Spring Rolls with Peanut Sauce pair well with a side of miso soup or a fresh green salad.

EGGPLANT STUFFED WITH NUT FILLING

Eggplant stuffed with nut filling is a classic Georgian* appetizer. Thin slices of eggplant are spread with a flavorful walnut and garlic filling, then rolled into delicious bites. This dish is perfect for any gathering and is sure to impress your guests.

NUTRITIVE VALUE PER SERVING (APPROXIMATE):

- **Calories:** 200 kcal
- **Carbs:** 10g / **Sugars:** 4g / **Fibers:** 5g
- **Proteins:** 4g
- **Fats:** 18g
- **GI:** Low

HERE IS HOW TO MAKE IT:

01 Preheat your oven to 375°F (190°C).

02 Slice the eggplants lengthwise into thin slices, about 1/4-inch thick.

03 Brush both sides of the eggplant slices with olive oil and season with salt and pepper.

04 Arrange the slices on a baking sheet and bake in the preheated oven for 15-20 minutes, until tender and slightly golden. Alternatively, you can grill the slices for a smoky flavor.

05 In a food processor, combine the chopped or ground walnuts, minced garlic, fresh cilantro, ground coriander, ground fenugreek, ground red pepper (if using), white wine vinegar, water, and salt. Process until smooth and well combined. The mixture should be spreadable; add more water if needed.

06 Allow the eggplant slices to cool slightly. Spread a thin layer of the nut filling onto each eggplant slice.

07 Roll up each slice tightly and place seam-side down on a serving platter.

08 Garnish with additional fresh cilantro if desired and serve at room temperature.

*not the U.S. Georgia, it's the country in the Caucasus.

PREP: 20 min   **COOK:** 20 min   **SERVINGS:** 4-6

INGREDIENTS YOU WILL NEED:

- 2 large eggplants (GI: 15)
- 1/4 cup olive oil (GI: 0)
- Salt and pepper to taste (GI: 0)

For the nut filling:

- 1 cup walnuts, finely chopped or ground (GI: 15)
- 2 garlic cloves, minced (GI: 30)
- 1/4 cup fresh cilantro, chopped (GI: 15)
- 1 teaspoon ground coriander (GI: 0)
- 1 teaspoon ground fenugreek (GI: 0)
- 1/2 teaspoon ground red pepper (optional) (GI: 0)
- 1 tablespoon white wine vinegar (GI: 0)
- 2 tablespoons water (GI: 0)
- Salt to taste (GI: 0)

INGREDIENTS SWAPS AND SUBSTITUTIONS:

- Add a touch of lemon juice to the filling for extra brightness.
- Use fresh parsley instead of cilantro if preferred.

SERVING SUGGESTIONS:

- Serve Eggplant Stuffed with Nut Filling as an appetizer or part of a mezze platter with other Georgian dishes. These rolls pair well with a variety of dips and fresh vegetable salads.

PREP: 20 min   **COOK:** 15 min   **SERVINGS:** 4

ZUCCHINI, FETA & SPINACH FRITTERS WITH GARLIC TZATZIKI

Zucchini, Feta, and Spinach Fritters with Garlic Tzatziki are a delicious and healthy option that makes a great appetizer or side dish. These fritters are packed with fresh vegetables and flavorful feta and perfectly complemented by a tangy garlic tzatziki sauce. They are sure to be a hit with everyone in the family.

NUTRITIVE VALUE PER SERVING (APPROXIMATE):

- **Calories:** 300 kcal
- **Carbs:** 10g / **Sugars:** 4g / **Fibers:** 2g
- **Proteins:** 18g
- **Fats:** 22g
- **GI:** Low

INGREDIENTS YOU WILL NEED:

For the fritters:

- 2 medium zucchinis, grated (GI: 15)
- 1 cup fresh spinach, chopped (GI: 15)
- 1/2 cup feta cheese, crumbled (GI: 30)
- 1/4 cup almond flour (GI: 25)
- 2 eggs, beaten (GI: 0)
- 2 garlic cloves, minced (GI: 30)
- 1 small onion, finely chopped (GI: 10)
- 1/4 cup fresh dill, chopped (GI: 25)
- 1/4 teaspoon salt (GI: 0)
- 1/4 teaspoon black pepper (GI: 0)
- 2 tablespoons olive oil (GI: 0)

For the garlic tzatziki:

- 1 cup Greek yogurt (GI: 35)
- 1 cucumber, grated and drained (GI: 15)
- 2 garlic cloves, minced (GI: 30)
- 1 tablespoon lemon juice (GI: 20)
- 1 tablespoon olive oil (GI: 0)
- 1 tablespoon fresh dill, chopped (GI: 25)
- Salt and pepper to taste (GI: 0)

HERE IS HOW TO MAKE IT:

01 Grate the zucchinis and place them in a clean kitchen towel. Squeeze out as much moisture as possible.

02 In a large bowl, combine the grated zucchini, chopped spinach, crumbled feta, almond flour, beaten eggs, minced garlic, chopped onion, fresh dill, salt, and black pepper. Mix well to combine.

03 Heat olive oil in a large skillet over medium heat.

04 Scoop 2 tablespoons of the mixture for each fritter into the skillet, flattening them slightly with a spatula.

05 Cook for 3-4 minutes on each side, or until golden brown and cooked through. Transfer to a paper towel-lined plate to drain any excess oil.

06 **Prepare the garlic tzatziki:** In a medium bowl, combine the Greek yogurt, grated and drained cucumber, minced garlic, lemon juice, olive oil, fresh dill, salt, and pepper. Mix well.

07 Serve the fritters warm with a generous dollop of garlic tzatziki on the side.

MEZE: EGGPLANT APPETIZER WITH YOGURT AND GARLIC

This Meze is a flavorful and healthy eggplant appetizer, perfect for serving with fresh vegetable sticks like cucumber, carrot, and celery. The creamy yogurt and garlic complement the roasted eggplant, making it a delightful dish for any occasion.

NUTRITIVE VALUE PER SERVING (APPROXIMATE):

- **Calories:** 150 kcal
- **Carbs:** 12g / **Sugars:** 5g / **Fibers:** 5g
- **Proteins:** 5g
- **Fats:** 10g
- **GI:** Low

PREP: 15 min   **COOK:** 40 min   **SERVINGS:** 4

HERE IS HOW TO MAKE IT:

01   Preheat your oven to 400°F (200°C).

02   Wash and dry the eggplants. Prick them a few times with a fork and place them on a baking sheet. Roast in the preheated oven for 35-40 minutes, turning occasionally, until the skin is charred and the flesh is tender.

03   Remove the eggplants from the oven and let them cool slightly. Once cool enough to handle, cut them in half and scoop out the flesh into a bowl. Discard the skins.

04   In the bowl with the eggplant flesh, add the Greek yogurt, minced garlic, olive oil, lemon juice, and chopped parsley. Mix well until combined. Season with salt and pepper to taste.

05   Transfer the mixture to a serving dish. Drizzle with a bit more olive oil and sprinkle with paprika, if using. Garnish with additional parsley if desired.

INGREDIENTS YOU WILL NEED:

- 2 large eggplants (GI: 15)
- 1 cup Greek yogurt (GI: 35)
- 3 garlic cloves, minced (GI: 30)
- 2 tablespoons olive oil (GI: 0)
- 1 tablespoon lemon juice (GI: 20)
- 1/4 cup fresh parsley, chopped (GI: 15)
- Salt and pepper to taste (GI: 0)
- 1/4 teaspoon paprika (optional) (GI: 0)

INGREDIENTS SWAPS AND SUBSTITUTIONS:

- Substitute Greek yogurt with dairy-free yogurt for a vegan option.
- Add a tablespoon of tahini for a richer flavor.
- Use cilantro instead of parsley for a different herb profile.

CHAPTER 15. GUILT-FREE BAKING & DIABETIC DESSERTS

Do you think having diabetes means saying goodbye to dessert? Think again! Whether you're insulin resistant or managing Type 2 diabetes, you can still enjoy sweet treats – the trick is moderation and food order.

The number one great tip is to eat your dessert after a fiber-rich, protein-packed meal. The protein, fiber, and healthy fats in your main course help stabilize blood sugar levels by slowing down glucose release and preventing those pesky sugar spikes.

Another way to control your blood sugar is to make desserts with ingredients rich in protein, fiber, and healthy fats. Think nuts, seeds, yogurt, and cottage cheese. These components ensure your sweet treats have a gentler impact on your blood sugar, helping you avoid dramatic spikes and drops.

Opt for ingredients with low or zero glycemic indexes and use natural sugar alternatives like Stevia, Erythritol, or Advantan. Stevia, in particular, might even help stabilize blood sugar levels and boost insulin production after meals.*

So go ahead, enjoy that dessert! With mindful ingredient choices and portion control, you can savor sweet treats without compromising your health.

*Before using sugar substitutes, consult your doctor; some can contain carbs and still raise your blood sugar. Using them in baking may require adjusting the recipe to your taste.

**In our recipes, we use Stevia as an example of a natural sugar substitute due to its additional beneficial properties, such as vitamins and antioxidants. However, some people might find its aftertaste slightly unpleasant; therefore, feel free to choose any other sugar alternative. Use available conversion charts relative to refined sugar to calculate the appropriate amounts.

***Ensure that the sugar substitute you choose retains its properties during heat processing.

HIGH-PROTEIN COTTAGE CHEESE BREAD WITH LINSEEDS AND SUNFLOWER SEEDS

This High-Protein Cottage Cheese Bread with Linseeds and Sunflower Seeds is a nutritious and delicious option for those looking to maintain a low-carb diet, especially beneficial for people with diabetes. The bread is rich in protein and healthy fats, which help stabilize blood sugar levels. Including linseeds and sunflower seeds not only adds a delightful crunch but also boosts the fiber content, promoting better digestive health.

NUTRITIVE VALUE PER SERVING (APPROXIMATE):

- **Calories:** 110 kcal
- **Carbs:** 4g / **Sugars:** 1g / **Fibers:** 2g
- **Proteins:** 7g
- **Fats:** 8g
- **GI:** Low

HERE IS HOW TO MAKE IT:

01 Preheat your oven to 350°F (175°C). Line a loaf pan with parchment paper.

02 In a large bowl, mix together the cottage cheese and eggs until well combined.

03 Add the almond flour, linseeds, sunflower seeds, baking powder, and salt to the wet mixture. Stir until all ingredients are evenly mixed.

04 Pour the batter into the prepared loaf pan and spread it out evenly.

05 Bake for 35-40 minutes, or until a toothpick inserted into the center comes out clean.

06 Allow the bread to cool in the pan for 10 minutes before transferring it to a wire rack to cool completely.

PREP: 15 min   **COOK:** 40 min   **SERVINGS:** 10

INGREDIENTS YOU WILL NEED:

- 1 cup cottage cheese (GI: 27)
- 3 large eggs (GI: 0)
- 1 cup almond flour (GI: 25)
- 1/2 cup linseeds (flaxseeds) (GI: 35)
- 1/2 cup sunflower seeds (GI: 35)
- 1 teaspoon baking powder (GI: 0)
- 1/2 teaspoon salt (GI: 0)

INGREDIENTS SWAPS AND SUBSTITUTIONS:

- If you wish to use coconut flour instead of almond flour, additional eggs may be needed due to coconut flour's high fiber content, and adjustments to the recipe may be required.

SERVING SUGGESTIONS:

- Enjoy this bread as a snack or for a hearty breakfast. Customize with herbs, spices, or other flavorings like garlic powder, onion powder, or grated cheese to suit your preferences.

PREP: 20 min **COOK:** 35-45 min **SERVINGS:** 10

LENTIL BREAD WITH FETA & SUNDRIED TOMATOES

Lentil Bread with Feta & Sundried Tomatoes is a nutritious and delicious option that is perfect for a healthy snack or a savory side dish. Packed with protein and rich flavors, this bread is both satisfying and wholesome.

NUTRITIVE VALUE PER SERVING (APPROXIMATE):

- **Calories:** 160 kcal
- **Carbs:** 18g / **Sugars:** 3g / **Fibers:** 6g
- **Proteins:** 9g
- **Fats:** 8g
- **GI:** Low

INGREDIENTS YOU WILL NEED:

- 2 cups red lentils, soaked overnight (GI: 35)
- 1/2 cup Greek yogurt (GI: 35)
- 3 large eggs (GI: 0)
- 1-2 teaspoons salt (GI: 0)
- 5 tablespoons olive oil (GI: 0)
- 1/3 cup crumbled feta cheese (GI: 30)
- 1/2 cup chopped sundried tomatoes (GI: 35)
- 2 tablespoons chopped fresh dill (GI: 25)
- 2 teaspoons baking powder (GI: 0)
- 1/2 teaspoon garlic powder (GI: 0)
- 1/2 teaspoon onion powder (GI: 0)
- 1 tablespoon sesame seeds (optional topping) (GI: 35)

INGREDIENTS SWAPS AND SUBSTITUTIONS:

- For a different flavor, you can replace feta cheese with goat cheese or add chopped olives for an extra Mediterranean twist.

SERVING SUGGESTIONS:

- Serve Lentil Bread with a side of fresh salad or as a savory addition to your favorite soup. It also makes a great base for sandwiches.

HERE IS HOW TO MAKE IT:

01 Wash and soak the lentils for at least one hour. Drain well.

02 Preheat your oven to 350°F (175°C) and line a 9×5 inch loaf pan with parchment paper.

03 Puree the lentils in a food processor until smooth.

04 In a large bowl, mix the lentil puree, Greek yogurt, eggs, and salt until well combined.

05 Add olive oil, feta cheese, sundried tomatoes, dill, baking powder, garlic powder, and onion powder. Stir until thoroughly mixed.

06 Pour the batter into the prepared loaf pan, smoothing the top. Tap the pan lightly to remove air bubbles. Sprinkle with sesame seeds if desired.

07 Bake for 35-45 minutes, or until a toothpick inserted into the center comes out clean.

08 Cool in the pan for 10 minutes, then transfer to a wire rack to cool completely.

HAZELNUT ALMOND BISCOTTI

Hazelnut Almond Biscotti is a delightful, crunchy treat perfect for people with diabetes. Made with almond flour and sweetened with stevia, these biscotti are a healthy, low-carb option that doesn't compromise flavor.

NUTRITIVE VALUE PER SERVING (APPROXIMATE):

- **Calories:** 80 kcal
- **Carbs:** 4g / **Sugars:** 1g / **Fibers:** 2g
- **Proteins:** 3g
- **Fats:** 6g
- **GI:** Low

HERE IS HOW TO MAKE IT:

01 Preheat your oven to 350°F (175°C). Line a baking sheet with parchment paper.

02 In a large bowl, combine almond flour, chopped hazelnuts, chopped almonds, stevia, baking powder, and salt. Mix well.

03 In a separate bowl, whisk together the eggs, vanilla extract, and almond extract until well combined.

04 Gradually add the wet ingredients to the dry ingredients, mixing until a dough forms.

05 Divide the dough in half and shape each half into a log about 10 inches long and 2 inches wide. Place the logs on the prepared baking sheet and flatten them slightly. Bake for 20-25 minutes, or until golden brown.

06 Remove from the oven and let the logs cool for about 10 minutes. Reduce the oven temperature to 300°F (150°C). Slice the logs diagonally into ½-inch thick slices.

07 Place the slices cut side down on the baking sheet. Bake for an additional 10-15 minutes, or until the biscotti are dry and crisp.

08 Allow the biscotti to cool completely on a wire rack before serving.

PREP: 20 min **COOK:** 35-40 min **SERVINGS:** 24

INGREDIENTS YOU WILL NEED:

- 2 cups almond flour (GI: 1)
- 1 cup chopped hazelnuts (GI: 15)
- 1/2 cup chopped almonds (GI: 15)
- 2 large eggs (GI: 0)
- 1 teaspoon vanilla extract (GI: 0)
- 1 teaspoon almond extract (GI: 0)
- 1 teaspoon stevia powder, equivalent to 1 cup sugar (GI: 0)
- 1 teaspoon baking powder (GI: 0)
- 1/4 teaspoon salt (GI: 0)

INGREDIENTS SWAPS AND SUBSTITUTIONS:

- For a different flavor, you can substitute the hazelnuts and almonds with other nuts like walnuts or pecans. Adding a teaspoon of cinnamon or a handful of sugar-free chocolate chips can also enhance the flavor profile.

SERVING SUGGESTIONS:

- Enjoy Hazelnut Almond Biscotti with a cup of coffee or tea. Packaged in a decorative tin or jar, these biscotti also make a great gift.

PREP: 15 min   **COOK:** 2 hours   **SERVINGS:** 12

NO-BAKE CHEESECAKE BARS

NUTRITIVE VALUE PER SERVING (APPROXIMATE):

- **Calories:** 200 kcal
- **Carbs:** 6g / **Sugars:** 2g / **Fibers:** 2g
- **Proteins:** 5g
- **Fats:** 18g
- **GI:** Low

HERE IS HOW TO MAKE IT:

01 Prepare the crust:

- In a bowl, combine almond flour, melted butter, and stevia. Mix until well combined.
- Press the mixture evenly into the bottom of a lined 8x8 inch baking dish.
- Chill in the refrigerator while preparing the filling.

02 Make the filling:

- In a large bowl, beat the softened cream cheese until smooth.
- Add Greek yogurt, stevia, vanilla extract, lemon juice, and lemon zest. Mix until well combined.

03 Assemble:

- Spread the cream cheese mixture evenly over the chilled crust.
- Evenly distribute the mixed berries over the cream cheese layer.

04 Chill:

- Refrigerate for at least 2 hours, or until set.

05 Serve:

- Cut into bars and enjoy!

INGREDIENTS YOU WILL NEED:

For the crust:
- 1 1/2 cups almond flour (GI: 25)
- 1/4 cup melted butter (GI: 14)
- 1/4 teaspoon of stevia powder, equivalent to 1/4 cup sugar (GI: 0)

For the filling:
- 16 oz cream cheese, softened (GI: 27)
- 1/2 cup Greek yogurt (GI: 35)
- 1/4 teaspoon of stevia powder, equivalent to 1/4 cup sugar (GI: 0)
- 1 teaspoon vanilla extract (GI: 0)
- 1 tablespoon lemon juice (GI: 20)
- Zest of 1 lemon (GI: 20)

For the topping:
- 1 cup mixed berries (raspberries, strawberries, blueberries) (GI: 25-40)

INGREDIENTS SWAPS AND SUBSTITUTIONS:

- For a vegan alternative, replace Greek yogurt with coconut yogurt. You can also top the bars with almond flakes or coconut shreds instead of mixed berries for a different texture and flavor.

SERVING SUGGESTIONS:

- These No-Bake Cheesecake Bars are perfect on their own or with a dollop of Greek yogurt or a sugar-free chocolate syrup.

COCONUT MILK PANNA COTTA

Panna Cotta is a classic Italian dessert known for its creamy texture and delicate flavor. Despite its name, which means "cooked cream" in Italian, the cream should never boil. This easy-to-make dessert can be served with various berries or sauces. In this recipe, we pair it with passion fruit puree and strawberry slices, adding a hint of lemon zest for extra freshness. We use only full-fat coconut milk, making it dairy-free and suitable for diabetics by using a sugar substitute.

NUTRITIVE VALUE PER SERVING (APPROXIMATE):

- **Calories:** 180 kcal
- **Carbs:** 10g / **Sugars:** 5g / **Fibers:** 2g
- **Proteins:** 4g
- **Fats:** 14g
- **GI:** Low to Medium

HERE IS HOW TO MAKE IT:

01 In a small bowl, sprinkle the gelatin over ¼ cup of water and let it bloom for about 5 minutes.

02 In a saucepan over medium heat, combine the coconut milk, stevia, vanilla extract, and lemon zest. Heat until the mixture is warm, but do not let it boil.

03 Add the bloomed gelatin to the saucepan and stir until completely dissolved.

04 Remove the mixture from heat and let it cool slightly.

05 Pour the mixture into four individual ramekins or serving glasses.

06 Refrigerate for at least 4 hours, or until set.

07 To serve, top each panna cotta with passion fruit puree and fresh strawberry slices.

PREP: 15 min **COOK:** 5min **CHILL:** 4 hours **SGS:** 4

INGREDIENTS YOU WILL NEED:

- 2 cups full-fat coconut milk (GI: 40)
- 1 tablespoon gelatin powder (GI: 0)
- 1/4 cup water (for blooming gelatin) (GI: 0)
- 1/4 teaspoon stevia powdered extract, equivalent to 1/4cup sugar (GI: 0)
- 1 teaspoon vanilla extract (GI: 0)
- Zest of 1 lemon (GI: 20)
- 1/2 cup passion fruit puree (GI: 30)
- Fresh strawberries, sliced (GI: 40)

INGREDIENTS SWAPS AND SUBSTITUTIONS:

- This Coconut Milk Panna Cotta can be enjoyed on its own or with a variety of toppings like fresh berries, a drizzle of sugar-free chocolate sauce, or a sprinkle of toasted coconut flakes.

SERVING SUGGESTIONS:

- For a different flavor profile, you can add a teaspoon of matcha powder or a few drops of almond extract to the mixture. If you prefer a different fruit topping, try using a raspberry or mango puree.

PREP: 20 min   **COOK:** 25-30 min   **SERVINGS:** 12

CREAM CHEESE SWIRL BROWNIES

Nothing beats a classic fudgy chocolate brownie, except maybe one that's swirled with creamy cheesecake! These Cream Cheese Swirl Brownies are not only delicious but also suitable for diabetics by using almond flour and stevia instead of sugar and regular flour.

NUTRITIVE VALUE PER SERVING (APPROXIMATE):

- **Calories:** 200 kcal
- **Carbs:** 6g / **Sugars:** 1g / **Fibers:** 3g
- **Proteins:** 5g
- **Fats:** 18g
- **GI:** Low

INGREDIENTS YOU WILL NEED:

For the brownie layer:
- 1 cup almond flour (GI: 25)
- 1/2 cup unsweetened cocoa powder (GI: 20)
- 1/2 teaspoon baking powder (GI: 0)
- 1/4 teaspoon salt (GI: 0)
- 1/2 cup melted butter or coconut oil (GI: 14)
- 3 large eggs (GI: 0)
- 1 teaspoon vanilla extract (GI: 0)
- 1 teaspoon stevia, equivalent to 1 cup sugar (GI: 0)

For the cream cheese swirl:
- 8 oz cream cheese, softened (GI: 20)
- 1 large egg (GI: 0)
- 1/4 teaspoon stevia, equivalent to 1/4 cup sugar (GI: 0)
- 1 teaspoon vanilla extract (GI: 0)

SERVING SUGGESTIONS:

- These Cream Cheese Swirl Brownies are perfect with whipped cream or fresh berries.

HERE IS HOW TO MAKE IT:

01 **Preheat and prepare:** preheat your oven to 350°F (175°C). Line an 8x8 inch baking pan with parchment paper or lightly grease it.

02 **Make the brownie layer:** in a medium bowl, whisk together almond flour, unsweetened cocoa powder, baking powder, and salt. In another bowl, combine melted butter or coconut oil, eggs, vanilla extract, and stevia. Mix until smooth. Gradually add the dry ingredients to the wet ingredients, mixing until well combined. Pour the brownie batter into the prepared baking pan, spreading it evenly.

03 **Make the cream cheese swirl:** in a separate bowl, beat the softened cream cheese until smooth. Mix the egg, stevia, and vanilla extract until well combined. Drop spoonfuls of the cream cheese mixture over the brownie batter. Use a knife or toothpick to swirl the cream cheese into the brownie batter, creating a marbled effect.

04 **Bake:** bake in the preheated oven for 25-30 minutes, or until a toothpick inserted into the center comes out mostly clean with a few moist crumbs.

05 **Cool and serve:** allow the brownies to cool in the pan for about 10 minutes before transferring them to a wire rack to cool completely. Cut into squares and enjoy!

BERRY OATMEAL CRISP

Packed with juicy berries, a hint of lemon, and a crunchy oat and pecan topping, this dessert is both satisfying and nutritious. Perfect for diabetics, it uses stevia as a sweetener and almond flour for an added health boost. For a delightful twist, the crisp can be easily adapted with different fruits like nectarines, plums, or apples.

NUTRITIVE VALUE PER SERVING (APPROXIMATE):

- **Calories:** 200 kcal
- **Carbs:** 18g / **Sugars:** 5g / **Fibers:** 5g
- **Proteins:** 4g
- **Fats:** 12g
- **GI:** Low to Medium

PREP: 15 min   **COOK:** 40 min   **SERVINGS:** 6

HERE IS HOW TO MAKE IT:

01 **Preheat and prepare:** preheat your oven to 350°F (175°C). Lightly grease an 8x8 inch baking dish.

02 **Make the filling:** in a large bowl, combine the mixed berries, lemon zest, lemon juice, stevia, and cornstarch. Stir until the berries are well coated. Pour the berry mixture into the prepared baking dish.

03 **Make the topping:** in a medium bowl, mix together the rolled oats, almond flour, chopped pecans, melted coconut oil, ground cinnamon, salt, and stevia until well combined.

04 **Assemble and bake:** evenly sprinkle the oat mixture over the berry filling. Bake in the preheated oven for 35-40 minutes, or until the topping is golden brown and the berries are bubbling.

05 **Cool and serve:** allow the crisp to cool for about 10 minutes before serving.

SERVING SUGGESTIONS:

- Serve this warm Berry Oatmeal Crisp with a dollop of Greek yogurt or a scoop of sugar-free vanilla ice cream for a delectable dessert experience.

INGREDIENTS YOU WILL NEED:

For the filling:

- 4 cups mixed berries (such as blueberries, raspberries, and strawberries) (GI: 25-40)
- Zest of 1 lemon (GI: 20)
- 1 tablespoon lemon juice (GI: 20)
- ¼ teaspoon stevia, equivalent to ¼ cup sugar (GI: 0)
- 1 tablespoon cornstarch (GI: 65)

For the topping:

- 1 cup old-fashioned rolled oats (GI: 55)
- 1/2 cup almond flour (GI: 25)
- 1/4 cup chopped pecans (GI: 10)
- 1/4 cup melted coconut oil (GI: 0)
- 1 teaspoon ground cinnamon (GI: 0)
- 1/4 teaspoon salt (GI: 0)
- 1/2 teaspoon stevia, equivalent to 2 tablespoons sugar (GI: 0)

INGREDIENTS SWAPS AND SUBSTITUTIONS:

- For a different flavor, substitute the berries with sliced nectarines, plums, or apples. Adjust the amount of sweetener to taste depending on the sweetness of the fruit used.

30-DAY MEAL PLAN

This meal plan allows flexibility in the sequence of days and dishes, and can be adjusted based on leftovers. It's an example of healthy meal combinations designed to ease your transition to new eating habits.

	BREAKFAST	LUNCH	DINNER
01	Protein-Packed Cottage Cheese Bagels with Salmon and Cucumber, *p.22*	• Tom Yum Soup with Zucchini Noodles, *p.31* • Sauteed Cabbage Asian Style, *p.55* • Garlic and Rosemary Duck Breast, *p.80*	• Avocado, Mango Salad With Arugula and Pine-Nuts, *p.35* • Baked Cod with White Beans, *p.85*
02	Zucchini Waffles with Crispy Bacon and Egg, *p.21*	• Quinoa & Veggie Salad With Zesty Tahini Lemon Dressing , *p.36* • Garlic Parmesan Crusted Chicken, *p.74*	• Peanut Turkey with Zucchini Noodles Thai Style, *p.77*
03	Greek Cottage Cheese Bowl, *p.28*	• Beet Salad with Goat Cheese, Arugula, and Creamy Mustard Dressing, *p.39* • Garlic Butter Quinoa, *p.51* • Herb-Crusted Rabbit Legs in Creamy Garlic Sauce, *p.67*	• Thai Beef Salad with Lime Dressing, *p.44*
04	Scrambled Tofu with Spinach and Tomatoes, *p.29*	• Soup with Porcini Mushrooms and Pearl Barley, *p.32* • No Pasta Vegetable Lasagna with Mozzarella and Tomato Salsa, *p.54*	• Roasted Red Peppers, Spinach & Mozzarella Stuffed Chicken, *p.75* • Zesty Garlic Sesame Green Beans, *p.56*
05	Green Shakshuka with Leeks and Spinach, *p.18*	• Mediterranean Chickpea Salad With Feta & Lemony Dressing, *p.43* • Classic Meatloaf with Ground Beef, Onions, and Eggs, *p.64*	• No Pasta Vegetable Lasagna with Mozzarella and Tomato Salsa, *p.54*
06	Nutritious Green Bean and Parmesan Omelet, *p.25*	• Gourmet Beef Burger with Portobello Mushrooms, Caramelized Onions, Blue Cheese, and Arugula, *p.69*	• Garlic Butter Shrimp with Zucchini Noodles & Cherry Tomatoes, *p.90*
07	Mushroom & Goat Cheese Breakfast Burritos, *p.20*	• Wild Rice Pilaf with Cranberries & Almonds, *p.50* • Indian Lamb Curry with Spinach and Spices, *p.65* • Pair with a salad, steamed, or grilled vegetables to taste	• Middle Eastern Roasted Eggplant Salad with Tahini Dressing, *p.42* • Asian-Inspired Duck Lettuce Wraps, *p.81*
08	Warm Quinoa Breakfast Bowl , *p.24*	• Spicy chicken breast and lentil soup, *p.34* • Cauliflower & Mushrooms Skillet, *p.53* • Turkey Meatloaf Muffins with Blue Cheese, *p.78*	• Orange and Herb Roasted Chicken Thighs, *p.73* • Strawberry, Avocado, Quinoa Salad with Pecan Brittle, *p.38*
09	Protein-Packed Cottage Cheese Bagels with Roasted Red Pepper and Basil Pesto, *p.22*	• Asian Cabbage Salad with Edamame, Almond Flakes, and Ginger Peanut Dressing, *p.45* • Stuffed Bell Pepper with Ground Beef, Quinoa, and Tomato Sauce, *p.61*	• Lemon Shrimp, Avocado & Tomato Salad, *p.40*
10	Spicy Tomato Egg Skillet, *p.17*	• Creamy Chicken Pan with Quinoa & Spinach, *p.72* • Pair with a salad, steamed, or grilled vegetables to taste	• Poached Salmon in Coconut Lime Sauce, *p.83* • Pair with a salad, steamed, or grilled vegetables to taste

However, it shouldn't complicate your life or significantly increase your weekly grocery budget. The main principles are to follow the correct meal order, eat plenty of fiber, and drink enough water throughout the day.

BREAKFAST	LUNCH	DINNER	
Cauliflower Hash Browns Served with Greek Yogurt, *p.27*	• Greek Moussaka with Eggplant, Ground Beef, and Bechamel, *p.62*	• Avocado, Mango Salad With Arugula and Pine-Nuts, *p.35* • Baked Cod with White Beans, *p.85*	11
Whole Grain Toast With Tuna & Egg Salad, *p.26*	• Tomato Seafood Soup, *p.33* • Herbs & Lemon Bulgur Pilaf, *p.52* • Mediterranean Sundried Tomato Chicken Meatballs, *p.76*	• Pepper & Garlic Crusted Sirloin Roast, *p.68* • Balsamic-Parmesan Sautéed Spinach, *p.57*	12
Protein-Packed Cottage Cheese Bagels with Sliced Turkey and Cranberry Sauce, *p.22*	• Baked Sweet Potato Italian Style, *p.58* • Shrimp & Asparagus Foil Pack, *p.86*	• Rainbow Lentil Stew With Parmesan, *p.48* • Italian Meatballs with Marinara Sauce and Parmesan, *p.63*	13
Zucchini Waffles with Crispy Bacon and Egg, *p.21*	• Turkey and Mushroom Stroganoff, *p.79* • Garlic Butter Quinoa, *p.51* • Pair with a salad, steamed, or grilled vegetables to taste	• Asparagus, Tomato Salad With Burrata Cheese, Pine-nuts & Balsamic Dressing, *p.41*	14
Nutritious Green Bean and Parmesan Omelet, *p.25*	• Pistachio Crusted Halibut , *p.88* • Quinoa & Veggie Salad With Zesty Tahini Lemon Dressing, *p.36*	• Peanut Turkey with Zucchini Noodles Thai Style, *p.77*	15
Greek Cottage Cheese Bowl, *p.28*	• Asian Cabbage Salad, *p.45* • Baked Chili Beans with Ground Beef, *p.70*	• Oven-Baked Salmon Greek Style, *p.89* • Pair with a salad, steamed, or grilled vegetables to taste	06
Protein-Packed Cottage Cheese Bagels with Mozzarella, Sun-Dried Tomatoes, and Basil, *p.22*	• Wild Rice Pilaf with Cranberries & Almonds, *p.50* • Ginger Beef Stir-Fry with Peppers, *p.66* • Pair with a salad, steamed, or grilled vegetables to taste	• Zucchini Philadelphia Roll, *p.93* • Sauteed Cabbage Asian Style, *p.55*	17
Scrambled Tofu with Spinach and Tomatoes, *p.29*	• Roasted Red Peppers, Spinach & Mozzarella Stuffed Chicken, *p.75* • Rainbow Lentil Stew With Parmesan, *p.48*	• Mediterranean Seafood Sauté, *p.87* • Baked Sweet Potato Italian Style, *p.58*	18
Mushroom & Goat Cheese Breakfast Burritos, *p.20*	• Stuffed Bell Pepper with Ground Beef, Quinoa, and Tomato Sauce, *p.61* • Avocado, Mango Salad With Arugula and Pine-Nuts, *p.35*	• Caprese Style Stuffed Avocado, *p.94* • One-Pan Coconut Chickpea Curry, *p.47*	19
Spicy Tomato Egg Skillet, *p.17*	• Asian Cabbage Salad, *p.45* • Thai Green Curry with Fish, *p.91* • Herbs & Lemon Bulgur Pilaf, *p.52*	• Gourmet Beef Burger with Portobello Mushrooms, Caramelized Onions, Blue Cheese, and Arugula, *p.69*	20

	BREAKFAST	LUNCH	DINNER
21	Tomato and Ricotta Omelet Bake in a Low-Carb Lentil Tortilla, *p.19*	• Cauliflower & Mushrooms Skillet, *p.53* • Garlic Parmesan Crusted Chicken, *p.74*	• Garlic Butter Shrimp with Zucchini Noodles & Cherry Tomatoes, *p.90*
22	Protein-Packed Cottage Cheese Bagels with Avocado and Red Pepper Flakes, *p.22*	• Porcini Mushroom Barley, *p.49* • Herb-Crusted Rabbit Legs in Creamy Garlic Sauce, *p.67* • Zesty Garlic Sesame Green Beans, *p.56*	• Turkey Meatloaf Muffins with Blue Cheese, *p.78* • Strawberry, Avocado, Quinoa Salad with Pecan Brittle, *p.38*
23	Warm Quinoa Breakfast Bowl, *p.24*	• Tom Yum Soup with Zucchini Noodles, *p.31* • Thai Beef Salad with Lime Dressing, *p.44*	• Tuna Patties with Lemon Caper Sauce, *p.84* • Middle Eastern Roasted Eggplant Salad with Tahini Dressing, *p.42*
24	Green Shakshuka with Leeks and Spinach, *p.18*	• Greek Moussaka with Eggplant, Ground Beef, and Bechamel, *p.62*	• Mediterranean Chickpea Salad With Feta & Lemony Dressing, *p.43*
25	Cauliflower Hash Browns Served with Greek Yogurt, *p.27*	• Quinoa & Veggie Salad With Zesty Tahini Lemon Dressing, *p.36* • Italian Meatballs with Marinara Sauce and Parmesan, *p.63*	• Sauteed Cabbage Asian Style, *p.55* • Pepper & Garlic Crusted Sirloin Roast, *p.68*
26	Protein-Packed Cottage Cheese Bagels with Peanut Butter & Blueberries, *p.22*	• Beet Salad with Goat Cheese, Arugula, and Creamy Mustard Dressing, *p.39* • Garlic and Rosemary Duck Breast, *p.80*	• Asparagus, Tomato Salad With Burrata Cheese, Pine-nuts & Balsamic Dressing, *p.41*
27	Zucchini Waffles with Crispy Bacon and Egg, *p.21*	• Tomato Seafood Soup, *p.33* • Pistachio Crusted Halibut, *p.88* • Pair with a salad, steamed, or grilled vegetables to taste	• Peanut Turkey with Zucchini Noodles Thai Style, *p.77*
28	Greek Cottage Cheese Bowl, *p.28*	• Shrimp & Asparagus Foil Pack, *p.86* • Baked Sweet Potato, *p.58*	• No Pasta Vegetable Lasagna with Mozzarella and Tomato Salsa, *p.54*
29	Whole Grain Toast With Tuna & Egg Salad, *p.26*	• Avocado, Mango Salad With Arugula and Pine-Nuts, *p.35* • Garlic Butter Quinoa, *p.51* • Turkey and Mushroom Stroganoff, *p.79*	• Mediterranean Sundried Tomato Chicken Meatballs, *p.76* • Pair with a salad, steamed, or grilled vegetables to taste
30	Warm Quinoa Breakfast Bowl , *p.24*	• Oven-Baked Salmon Greek Style, *p.89* • Pair with a salad, steamed, or grilled vegetables to taste	• Zucchini, Feta & Spinach Fritters with Garlic Tzatziki, *p.98*

Made in the USA
Columbia, SC
23 November 2024